Stock Market Investing for Beginners:

Essentials to Start Investing Successfully

Table of Contents

Introduction
Chapter 1: Stocks 101

What is a stock?
The stock market
Is it gambling?
Short term vs. long term
The truth behind the myths

- Investing in stocks is a quick and easy way to make money
- Investing in stocks is only for the rich
- To be successful, you need to have special connections
- Investing in stocks will make you an instant millionaire
- Investing in stocks is safe and risk-free
- Investing in stocks will only make you lose all your money

Risks

- Market risk
- Economic risk
- Legal risk
- Headline risk
- Commodity price risk
- Interest risk and inflation

Benefits

- Profitable
- Convenient
- You are the boss
- Financial freedom
- It's fun

Stock trading broker

- Latest reviews
- Banking
- Trading or Investment platform
- Fees
- Minimum and maximum amount per investment
- Mobile feature

- Customer support
- Demo account

Trading psychology

- Greed
- Fear
- Regret
- Overconfidence
- Winning mindset

Chapter 2: Stock Trading Strategies

- **Fundamental analysis**
- **Technical analysis**
- **Averaging down**
- **Growth investing**
- **Value investing**
- **Stock split**
- **Stock mastery**
- **Develop your own**

Chapter 3: Best Practices

- Research
- Start small
- Write a trading or investing journal
- Cash out
- Take a break
- Continuous improvement
- Diversify your risks
- Professional approach

Chapter 4: Mistakes to Avoid

- Chasing after your losses
- Using an untested strategy
- Relying completely on expert advice
- Taking weak trading positions
- Being a victim of the 'pump and dump' scheme
- Trading aggressively

Conclusion

© Copyright 2018 by _____ - All rights reserved.

The transmission, duplication, or reproduction of any of the following work including specific information will be considered an illegal act irrespective of whether it is done electronically or in print. This extends to creating a secondary or tertiary copy of the work or a recorded copy and is only allowed with the express written consent from the Publisher. All additional rights reserved.

The information in the following pages is broadly considered to be a truthful and accurate account of facts, and as such any inattention, use, or misuse of the information in question by the reader will render any resulting actions solely under their purview. There are no scenarios in which the publisher or the original author of this work can be, in any fashion, deemed liable for any hardship or damages that may befall them after undertaking information described herein. The author does not take any responsibility for inaccuracies, omissions, or errors which may be found therein.

Additionally, the information in the following pages is intended only for informational purposes and should thus be thought of as universal. As befitting its nature, it is presented without assurance regarding its prolonged validity or interim quality. The author of this work is not responsible for any loss, damage, or inconvenience caused as a result of reliance on information as published on, or linked to, this book.

The author of this book has taken careful measures to share vital information about the subject. May its readers acquire the right knowledge, wisdom, **inspiration**, and succeed.

Introduction

Congratulations on downloading this book and thank you for doing so.

If you want to leave your 8-hour job and be your own boss, or if you simply want to find a way to increase your monthly income, then you should definitely consider investing in the stock market. By trading stocks, you can earn a high amount of income, even a full-time income. Not to mention, you can enjoy and earn all the profits that you can make from the comfort of your home.

Thanks to the convenience of modern technology, you can start investing in stocks with just a few clicks of the mouse. The real challenge lies in picking the right stocks to invest in. The unfortunate truth is that there are so many people who invest stocks without even understanding what they are doing. The activity of successfully investing in stocks for profit takes so much more than just randomly choosing stocks and hoping for a favorable outcome. In order to be successful, you have to learn and master the basics and use effective trading strategies to turn the odds in your favor. Indeed, given the right foundation and understanding, you can turn the stock market into a goldmine of profits.

The following chapters will teach you the ins and outs of investing in stocks for profit:

- Chapter 1 discusses the basics. Learn about what a 'stock is' and how the stock market works, among many others. This chapter will give you the foundation that you need to be successful

- Chapter 2 teaches the amazing stock investing and trading strategies that you can use to turn the odds in your favor

- Chapter 3 lays down the best practices that you should observe to increase your chances of making a profit

- Chapter 4 talks about the mistakes that you should avoid. You should take note of these pitfalls to avoid committing the same mistakes that many other people did

There are plenty of books on this subject on the market, so thanks again for choosing this one! Every effort was made to ensure it is full of as much useful information as possible. Please enjoy!

Chapter 1: Stocks 101

Before we go into the technical aspects of investing or trading stocks, you should first have a good understanding of the basics. The basics will serve as your foundation, which is very important to your success. This is also a good way to know just what you should expect. Let us discuss them one by one:

What is a stock?

The term 'stock' refers to the ownership of a company. It is also referred to as a 'share of stock' or simply 'share.' Once you buy stocks of a company, you become entitled to the rights of ownership of said company, and this includes rights over the company's earnings, assets, and voting rights. Also, the word 'stocks' is just a general term. Stocks have various classifications, such as common stocks, redeemable stocks, treasury stocks, and many others. But, when you hear investors talk about stocks, they almost always refer to 'common stocks.'

The stock market

The 'stock market' refers to the place or platform where stocks are traded. This is where the buying and selling of stocks take place. The stock market also reflects the economic conditions. This is because when the economy is well, the prices of stocks also tend to increase. However, when the economy is not doing well, then the prices of stocks tend to suffer. Hence, a good tip to determine how good or bad a certain economy is doing is by looking at the behavior of the prices of stocks. Now, keep in mind that the prices of stocks do not just move at random. Stocks are owned mostly by businesses. If the business is doing well, then the prices of stocks increase. However, when the business is not doing well, then the prices of stocks tend to decrease. Okay, you might be wondering: "Why do companies offer their stocks to the public?" The reason here is that by offering stocks to the market, companies can finance their business. After all, in order for you to own a stock, you have to pay for it. By offering stocks, companies can accrue the necessary funds for the expansion and further development of the business. After all, money is the lifeblood of a business.

Is it gambling?

"So, is it gambling?" This is something that many people wonder. The reason why this question usually remains unanswered is because that there is no clear-cut answer to it. This depends on how you approach the activity of investing in or trading stocks. If you approach the market by simply relying on guesswork and assuming that luck is on your side, then you are gambling. In this case, investing in stocks becomes a gamble. However, if every action that you make is backed up by solid research and analysis, and if you consider every position you make as an investment decision, then you are investing and not gambling.

Also, just because there are risks involved in this activity that does not mean that it is gambling. After all, everything has its risks. Even businesses have to deal with many risks and challenges. What is important is how you approach it and how you turn that opportunity that you see into actual profit. So, is investing in stocks a gamble? Well, it depends on you. However, as much as this book is concerned, we discourage relying on luck. Do not gamble. In order to increase your chances of attaining success and enjoy a continuous flow of profits, you should take the time and effort to study the market and apply effective strategies.

Short term vs. long term

When you invest in stocks, you are in control of your investment. This means that you can invest in them for as long as you want or for a short period. At some point in the future, if you feel like closing your position to enjoy your profits, then you can easily do so with just a click of the mouse. Investments in stocks can be divided into two classifications: short-term and long-term investments. There is no clear rule to determine what makes an investment short or long. However, many agree that if the investment is held for longer than a year, then that is a long-term investment, while investments that are held for less than a year are considered short-term investments.

There is also what is known as 'day trading.' As the name suggests, this is trading stocks in one trading day. It is a kind of short-term investment. Day traders are active and make multiple trades in a day. When you day trade, you open your positions and close them at the end of the trading day. You can then start with a clean slate the following day, hence, the term 'day trading.'

Now, it should be noted that the prices of stocks do not fluctuate heavily, unless if you invest in penny stocks, which are much riskier. This means that if you only invest for a few days or weeks, then you might barely see any significant changes in the value of your investment. People who engage in short-term trades, like day traders, normally have a high capital, so a small percentage of gain or loss can have a significant impact on their investment.

So, which is better? A short-term or a long-term investment? Well, none is better than the other. It will depend on your approach and the strategy that you will use. So, just do what you think is the best and most suitable for you. If you are just starting out, then you might want to try both and see what happens. Whether you trade for a short-term or a long-term is up to you to decide.

The truth behind the myths

There are various myths related to stock investing. For you to have a better understanding of the stock market and what it means to be an investor, then you have to know the truth behind these myths:

Investing in stocks is a quick and easy way to make money

Although investing in stocks can make you rich, it is not something that you can easily achieve overnight. Keep in mind that the prices of stocks do not fluctuate rapidly. So, do not expect to make a multi-million profit in just one day. Normally, it takes time to earn a significant amount of income when you invest in stocks. If you invest just a few dollars, then it will surely take some time before you can earn your first million. It is also not easy to make money by investing in stocks since it takes time and considerable effort for you to identify the right stocks to invest in. You cannot just rely on mere guesswork. You have to take action and actually study the market if you want to make a large profit. Just like any other investment or business, investing in stocks also demands continuous research and practice. You need to learn and apply effective strategies. You also need to be flexible enough and be ready for abrupt changes in the market. All in all, participating in the stock market can be challenging, but it is nonetheless, very rewarding.

Investing in stocks is only for the rich

Although it is true that there are wealthy people who invest in stocks, it is also true that many stock traders and investors are 'low rollers' or the people who only have a few hundred or thousand dollars in their trading account. The thing is, it is very easy to enter the stock market. If you are of legal age, have an Internet connection and a decent computer, and if there is no legal restriction in your country, then you can easily start investing in stocks. What's more, you can do all of this from the comfort of your home.

In case you didn't know, a majority of the people who consider themselves to be stock investors are not rich. In fact, the reason why they invest in stocks is not because that they are already rich but because they want to become rich. Now, different stock brokers may have different requirements or guidelines, but most brokers will allow you to start investing in stocks even with just a hundred dollars in your account.

To be successful, you need to have special connections
Although it can be quite an advantage if you have some sort of special connections that can help you come up with a profitable investment decision, this is not always the case. Getting inside information can only be beneficial to a certain extent, but it does not guarantee any favorable outcome. It should also be noted that nobody can guarantee the direction that the market is going to take. There are so many things that can happen, and many of which are outside of anyone's control. Although it can be an advantage if you have some special connections, you can still invest in stocks successfully on your own.

Investing in stocks will make you an instant millionaire
It is true that investing in stocks can make you a millionaire, but do not think that it will be fast and easy. In fact, a percentage profit of 20% in a year is already considered good enough. If you want to earn more money, then you will have to invest a bigger amount of funds.

Investing in stocks is safe and risk-free
In any investment, there are always some risks involved. This is also true when you invest in stocks. Many people who invest in stocks without taking the time and effort to understand the market end up losing all their capital in the long run. Hence, before you make any investment in stocks, be sure that you understand how it works and that you have thoroughly researched the market.

Investing in stocks will only make you lose all your money
There are also people who believe that if you invest in stocks, you will only lose your money in the long run. Again, you have to understand that you should not approach the stock market as a gamble. If you take the time and effort to closely study the market and apply effective strategies, then you can significantly increase your chances of making a large profit. Remind yourself that this is an investment. Just like any other investments, there are risks involved, but there is also that one golden opportunity to make it big.

Risks

Let us now discuss the risks involved when you invest in stocks. It is important that you be aware of these so that you will know just what to expect.

- **Market risk**
  Market risk refers to the people. When you say that you invest in stocks, it does not mean that your only concern would be the stocks alone. Do not forget that stocks move because of people. Hence, it is also important that you learn how to understand people for you to know what direction that the market is going to take. Unfortunately, the market has its own preferences and prejudices. What is more, people can have different opinions. Indeed, it is not that easy to learn how to read the market and know how the people would respond to certain changes. It is possible that the best stock to invest in today may no longer be considered a profitable choice by tomorrow. This is because of the basic rule that people change, including their preferences. Hence, when you invest in stocks, it is important that you keep a close eye on the market and analyze how it moves and responds.

- **Economic risk**
  As already stated, the economy is one of the factors that affect the prices of stocks. In fact, the economy mirrors the situation of the stocks. Hence, if businesses and stocks are doing well, then the economy also improves. But, when the stocks and businesses are down, then this situation is reflected in the economy. Another challenging part is that there are certain things about the economy that is outside anyone's control. A good example of this would be the terrorist attack that took place in 2001. It made the economy suffer, and it resulted in a decrease in the prices of different stocks in the market. When this happens, you might be able to just ride out the bad streak, but there are times that the blow inflicted on the market is too great to recover from and leads to collapse.

- **Legal risk**
  This risk is mostly related to the relationship between the government and businesses. The government may enact laws that can affect the standing of businesses. There is the risk that the government might suddenly enact a law that can adversely affect a business. When this happens, and if the business concerned fails to handle it properly, then the prices of its stocks might drop. Laws may be enacted that can restrict or limit business practices. Of course, governments are not against businesses. After all, businesses are important to the economy. However, the government can enact laws to secure and protect the welfare of its people. Unfortunately, sometimes the exercise of this power and prerogative can adversely affect certain businesses.

- **Headline risk**
  This pertains to the risk of being negatively featured on the news. In a way, this functions like a negative promotion. This does not just refer to the traditional news, but anything that can go viral like social media. Because of the tight competition, some businesses resort to dishonest and unfair practices. If a negative promotion gains much attention, then it can influence the market, which is not good for a business. Of course, this can affect the price of its stocks in a negative way.

- **Commodity price risk**
  This refers to the risk in the price of certain commodities. Sometimes the prices of commodities change. Although this is good if the price increases, it is not good for businesses if it results in the price decreasing. It should also be noted that even if a company does not deal with the subject of commodities, it is still affected by this risk. This is because when the price of certain commodities change, then it also affects the purchasing power of the people. Needless to say, this can affect many other businesses, as well as their stocks. As you can see, this risk can affect the whole economy. As you already know, the economy has a close connection to the price of stocks.

- **Interest risk and inflation**
  For businesses that need financing, interest risk matters a lot. Of course, a higher rate would mean more problems for a business. As the rate that a business has to pay increases, it will be harder for it to stay in the game and make a profit for its own. Now, you can combine this with the risk of inflation. Combine these two, and you can find a trap that would be difficult for a business to get out of. Worse, if the economy also falls, then it would be almost impossible for any struggling business to survive.

Benefits

Now that you know the associated benefits of investing in stocks and if you think that you are still up for it, then it is time for you to know the wonderful benefits of investing in or trading stocks:

- **Profitable**
  Of course, the number one reason why people invest in stocks is because that it is a profitable investment. Although there are risks involved, once you get used to the market and develop a good understanding of how it works, then you can turn the stock market into a goldmine. In fact, there are people who have left their 8-hour office job and now invest in stocks as a full-time career. Indeed, if you get good at investing in stocks, then you can earn a high amount of profit from it.

- **Convenient**
  Thanks to modern technology, you can easily invest in stocks from the comfort of your own home. All you need is access to the Internet, and you can start using some trading platforms. Once you work as a stock investor, you can enjoy working while lying in bed, wearing nothing but your pajamas. Making trades and investments is also fast and simple, and all it takes is just a few clicks of the mouse.

- **You are the boss**
  If you are tired of always having to please your boss and doing whatever he or she tells you, then becoming a stock investor might just be the path for you. When you engage in stock investment, you become your own boss. You do not have to wake up early in the morning or do things you do not want to do. You take full control of everything. However, just be careful. As the saying goes, "With great power comes great responsibility." Just as you are the boss, you are also responsible for everything. If you get too lazy to study the market or become too careless, then the chances are that you might lose your investment. Still, you are the boss. Just be sure to be responsible enough so that you will not regret it.

- **Financial freedom**
  Indeed, there is no better way to obtain financial freedom than making money work for you. Normally, people work for money. However, successful investors know better. They know that the secret to financial freedom is to make money work for you instead. You can only do this by making an investment. Now, when it comes to investments, one of the best investments that you can make is putting your funds in profitable stocks and watching them grow. Indeed, becoming a successful stock investor is an excellent way to attain financial freedom. It is time for you to stop being a slave working for money. By becoming a stock investor, you can make money work for you.

- **It's fun**
  It cannot be denied that the activities of a stock investor can be really fun. In fact, many investors do not notice the time pass them by as they enjoy coming up with sound investment decisions. It can be fun to follow up on the market

and find out if your last positions gained any profit. Of course, it is really nice and exciting every time you see that you have made a profit just by choosing the right stocks to invest in. You are not just your own boss, you can also be a highly successful person.

Stock trading broker

Before you can start investing in stocks, you need to open an account with a broker first. Now, by simply using your favorite search engine, you will find a long list of different brokers that offer the same service and allow you to invest in stocks. You need to choose the broker that will best suit your needs. More importantly, you need to work only with a trustworthy and reliable broker. Unfortunately, there are so many scammers and hackers online. So, how do you identify the broker that is right for you? Here are the criteria that you should consider:

Latest reviews

Before you deposit your hard-earned money into your account, be sure to check the latest reviews given to the stockbroker. You can do this easily by using your favorite browser. Simply type the name of the broker followed by the word 'reviews.' The 'Search Engine Result Pages' (SERP) will then show you related pages. Read as many reviews as you can and compare them with the reviews given to other brokers.

You should also pay attention to the dates when the reviews were made. If the last reviews were made about a year ago, then you should exercise more caution. Do not forget that the management team can change and how the broker handles its operations can also change. Also, it's worth keeping in mind that just because a broker has many positive reviews, that does not necessarily mean that you should no longer exercise caution when you're dealing with them. You should be diligent at all times. The positive reviews can only help to make you feel more confident about working with a broker, but it does not guarantee that the said broker will not scam or treat you unfairly. Always exercise caution.

Banking

Before you put money into your account, you should check the banking page or information of the broker first. It is not rare to find brokers that have more options for making a deposit and only a few limited options for making a withdrawal. Hence, before you deposit any money, be sure that you take note of the deposit and withdrawal methods acceptable to your broker. Otherwise, you run the risk of having your funds locked in your account without any way of withdrawing them. If this matter is not clear to you, do not hesitate to contact the customer support team.

It should also be noted that it is common for brokers to require certain documents, mostly documents that verify your identity, like a valid ID and billing statement before it processes a withdrawal request. Be sure that you have the required documents in your possession and that they have not yet expired. Most brokers are strict with the processing of withdrawals, so be sure that you understand this clearly.

Brokers normally restrict the withdrawal method to the deposit method that you use. For example, if you deposit via PayPal, then you should also withdraw your funds using PayPal. Of course, not all brokers have this limitation, so be sure to check it out before you make any substantial deposits into your account.

Trading or Investment platform
Of course, it is your broker that will provide you with the trading or investment platform that you will use to buy and sell stocks. The platform should make the experience of trading easy and convenient for you. It should also provide you with tools like graphs and other important data to help you come up with a sound investment decision. It should also be professionally designed. Although the design may not be considered by others to be necessary, it is still helpful as it helps set you in the right mood for investing. Again, the platform provided by your broker should help you make investments and give you a convenient experience.

Fees
Brokers may charge fees for certain transactions, such as a trading fee (which is a fee imposed per trade), surcharges, and withdrawal fees, among others. You should look for a reliable broker that charges the lowest rate possible. Although the fees may just be small amounts, they can easily pile up into a big amount. This is true, especially if you intend to make multiple trades in a week.

If you want to engage in day trading, then you can expect to make multiple trades in a day. Therefore, you should pay attention to the fees that are being charged by your broker. The fees may differ from broker to broker, so be sure to make a comparison. Needless to say, when it comes to choosing a broker, it would take much more than just finding out the one with the lowest fee. You should focus more on finding a reliable and trustworthy broker, a broker that will not rip you off and run away with your money. This is one of the reasons why you should only work with popular brokers who have positive reviews.

Minimum and maximum amount per investment

Knowing the minimum and maximum amount that you can invest is also important to know what kind of strategy that you should use. Knowing the minimum amount per investment or trade is also important especially if you are working on a low budget.

Mobile feature

These days, it is much more convenient to access the Internet using your mobile device. Brokers know about this, so they often come up with a mobile version of their platform. Do not worry, most, if not all, trustworthy brokers offer a mobile version that will allow you to make investments using your phone or tablet.

The mobile version may not allow you to access all the features of the site. This is normal. But, it should allow you to do important actions such as buying and selling stocks, as well as making a deposit or requesting for a withdrawal. A trading or investment platform with a mobile application is a must these days as it not only makes the process of investing in stocks more convenient, but it also allows you to invest in stocks virtually anywhere by just using your mobile device.

Customer support

When you work with a broker, especially if you intend to work with them for a long time, then it is strongly advised that you choose a broker that has an active and helpful customer support department. The customer support will help you with any technical issues that you may have with the site, as well as any other related questions that you might have in the future. Find out how to get in touch with the support team. Normally, there is a separate page on the platform where you can send customer support a message. Some brokers even provide a number that you can call, as well as an on-page chat feature, while others might only provide you with an email address. One way you can find out how helpful the customer support is by testing them. You can do this by sending an inquiry to the support team and check just how well it handles your inquiry. Normally, you should get a response from the support team within 24 hours.

Demo account

Most brokers will provide you with a demo account. Using a demo account is an excellent way to have a real market experience without risking any real money. Of course, you will also not earn any money from it, but it is a good and safe way to gain experience.

Even if you are already a well-experienced investor, you can still benefit from a demo account. A demo account can be helpful with testing your strategy in the market. After all, the life of a stock investor is mostly about developing your winning strategy. Having a demo account can save you from losing money as you look for that winning strategy.

Trading psychology

What is 'trading psychology?' Well, it simply refers to the mindset of a trader or investor. This is important since your mindset plays an important role in your success. You should be aware of the different mindsets, especially the ones that you should avoid to help minimize your risks and losses. Remember that your mindset is crucial to your success.

Greed

Greed is often the main reason why many investors lose their money. Although you invest in stocks to earn a profit, you should keep your desire under control. Investors lose their money not because they failed to pick the right stocks, but because they held on to those for too long. Do not forget that the stock market is volatile. This means that the prices of stocks are susceptible to change. They rise and fall continuously. You want to hold on to a position when the price is going up, and you must be disciplined enough to let go of it before the price drops.

Fear

This is the opposite of greed. Because of fear, investors fail to make good investments. Accept the fact that there will always be risks involved no matter how hard you study the market. It is your job to strike a balance between fear and greed. To combat fear, you need to gain more knowledge and learn how to apply an effective strategy.

Regret

Regret is when you miss out on a good investment. Do not worry, this is normal. Every time that you experience this, simply learn from the experience. Remember, there is always a lesson to be learned from the things we regret. This also happens when you commit a mistake and lose a position. Again, do not be discouraged. Simply learn from it. After all, you will surely commit mistakes every now and then. The important thing is to learn from your experience and use your knowledge to become a better investor. The more that you learn, the more profits that you can make.

Overconfidence

Although having confidence is good, too much confidence is a sure way to lose all of your money. Be sure to keep your confidence in check. A common mistake is to start doing less research after experiencing a series of profitable investments. Remember, don't ever let down your defenses. Instead, you should continue to work hard, if not harder. Always study the market, and never make any investment without sufficient research.

Winning mindset

The 'winning mindset' refers to a person who does not submit to fear or greed. An important part of having this winning mindset is to have self-discipline. Now, this may surprise you, but a person with a true winning mindset does not focus so much on the money. This is because someone with a winning mindset has already realized that money will come as long as you continue to make the right investment decisions. Instead of focusing on the money, focus on the facts and circumstances of the stock market. By doing so, you can increase your chances of choosing the right stocks to invest in.

A person with a winning mindset also knows that continuous success takes time, dedication, and effort. If you want to keep on making profits, then you should keep on working. Hence, you need to continue studying the stock market and develop a winning strategy.

You should also not panic even during a market collapse. Panicking will only lead to you making more wrong decisions. Instead, you should always be in control of your emotions. Don't submit to fear and panic. Learn to stop, relax, and view the market from a clear and calm perspective. This way you can come up with better decisions.

A person with a winning mindset also knows that in order to be successful, you need to take some risks. However, this is not just freely taking all kinds of risks but calculated risks. This refers to a risk that you can handle. A person with a winning mindset also knows how to handle losing trades or investments. After all, in the long course of making investments, it cannot be avoided that you will also encounter the bitterness of losing your positions. However, remember that what is important is not always winning every position that you have, but making a profit once you put everything together. A person with a winning mindset also knows the importance of positive thinking but remains reasonable and logical. They do not delude themselves and come up with practical solutions and actions. Last but not the least, a person with a winning mindset does not give up and always looks for ways to improve.

Building a winning mindset does not happen overnight. It is a result of continuous study and practice. Do not rush the development process, and try to learn as much as you can. Continue to improve yourself and be the best investor that you can be.

Chapter 2: Stock Trading Strategies

You cannot achieve a consistent flow of profits just by relying on luck. To significantly increase your chances of success, you should use effective strategies. Take note that just reading about these strategies is not enough. Investing in stocks is like learning a new skill. You also need to practice it. Let us discuss some of the notable strategies that you should know:

Fundamental analysis

Fundamental analysis is also referred to as the 'lifeblood' of investment. Hence, this is definitely something that is worth learning. This strategy does not just apply to the stock market but also in all kinds of investment. So, what is fundamental analysis? Fundamental analysis studies the fundamentals or the basics. As such, it is very important. You are probably familiar with the saying, "Knowledge is power." Well, this is what this strategy is all about. When you use this strategy, you should research and analyze the different factors that affect a stock or the stock market in general, such as the economy, level of competition, legalities, as well as market acceptance, among other things.

When you use this strategy, it is important that you follow up on the latest news since the news reveals important information about the stock market. Although fundamental analysis might be the strategy that demands the most time and effort, it is also highly effective. If you are serious about being a successful stock investor, then you should definitely learn about this strategy. In fact, successful investors use this daily. As a professional investor, you need to be up-to-date with the latest developments in the stock market.

It is also worth noting that fundamental analysis can be used along with another strategy. This strategy is not just about gathering all kinds of information. Rather, it has to be high-quality and reliable information. Of course, you also need to do your own analysis to identify the best information. You will soon realize that the more that you know about the market and the different stocks, the more likely it is that you will come up with the right investment decisions.

Technical analysis

If you are the visual type of person, then you might find this strategy interesting. Technical analysis makes use of graphs and charts to study the price movements of a particular stock. The idea behind this strategy is that the different factors that can affect a stock have their final effect on its price. Therefore, just by analyzing the price movements of a stock, you also get to deal with all the factors that influence it. You might want to consider this as the simplified and visual version of fundamental analysis.

When you use this strategy, you should learn to read patterns. Okay, you might be wondering: "Do patterns really exist?" The answer is 'yes.' In fact, even a random generator creates patterns. However, it should be noted that patterns come and go. What this means is, you cannot expect to see a pattern all of the time. There will be times when no matter how hard you study a graph, there is simply no pattern to be seen. Again, you don't need to worry because this is normal. A common mistake is forcing yourself to see a pattern even when no pattern exists. Remember, always make your analysis with a clear and unbiased mind. It is better for you not to proceed with making a decision than forcing yourself to see something which isn't even there.

Just like fundamental analysis, technical analysis can be used together with another strategy. In fact, many expert traders use both fundamental and technical analysis at the same time. Indeed, the more information that you have, the more likely it is that you can come up with the right investment decision. Technical analysis is an excellent strategy for short-term investments, but it can also be used for long-term investments.

Averaging down

This strategy will allow you to purchase stocks at a bargain. You can then sell them for profit. The best way to explain how this works is by using an example. Let us say, you want to buy the stocks of company X, and its current price is $10 per stock. You then make a buy order at the said rate. If its price increases, then you can easily sell it for profit. Now, if the price decreases, then according to this strategy, you should make another buy order. So, if the price drops, say, to $9, then you should make a buy order at $9. Now, if the price decreases again, then make another buy order at the lower price. This way you are buying stocks at a much lower price.

Okay, you might be wondering: "Are you not simply buying a losing stock?" Although it may look like it, this is not actually the case. In fact, you are making a sound investment. Just imagine how much profit you could make once the price of the stock goes back to its original price (its price when you first applied the strategy) or higher. All the buy orders that you have made will give you a nice return on your initial investment.

Now, it should be noted that this approach is considered highly aggressive, so be very careful every time you use it. The key here is to identify a stock that will most likely increase in price. Take as much time as you can to research the stock concerned, as your success will depend on whether its price will increase or at least recover in the near future.

A good strategy to use together with averaging down is fundamental analysis or technical analysis. You cannot use averaging down alone on its own as it relates only to the amount that you invest and does not tell you where to make an investment. Of course, where you put your money in is a crucial factor when it comes to making profitable investments. This strategy will allow you to weather fluctuations in the market since you're holding on to profitable stock investments. Again, keep in mind that although this seems highly practical, it is still considered a highly aggressive approach.

Growth investing

This is where you invest in the stocks of a company because you believe that the company has a potential to grow. This is usually used for small and start-up companies since they have room for development. When you use this strategy, take a look at new businesses. Consider how they are positioned in the market. Can they match up with the competition? Do not just focus on the company. Keep in mind that the strengths and weaknesses of a business are relative to the strengths and weaknesses of its competitors. Therefore, you should also keep an eye on competing businesses. This is a good way to gauge how a particular business is doing in the market. It is not enough that a company has space to grow, but the business should take positive actions to grow even further. Last but not the least, you should also pay attention to market acceptance. After all, no matter how amazing a business is, it would not do any good if the market ignores it or simply does not accept what it offers. These are the important things to consider when you use this strategy. The drawback of using this strategy is that since you will most likely be dealing with start-up companies, there may not be enough information that you could use to measure the profitability of these companies. This is a challenge that you have to overcome with this strategy.

Value investing

This is similar to growth investing. However, in this case, it is the value that you need to look into. When you use this strategy, you should look for a company that offers its stocks at a price that is lower than their actual value. Okay, this is where the challenge is. It is you who will have to determine the value of their stocks of the company. You need to look for stocks that are underpriced in the market. The idea behind this strategy is that the value of the stocks will soon adjust and correct itself. When this happens, and if you find a company that is underpriced, then you will soon gain a nice profit. Unlike growth investing, value investing does not just work on new companies. It can also apply to old companies or stocks. Still, this is a good strategy to use on new and start-up companies since they tend to have good value but have a low stock price. It is good to use this strategy together with fundamental analysis. Take as much time as you need to study the company. Of course, do not forget to compare its strengths and weaknesses with the strengths and weaknesses of its competitors. If you find a company that has good value but is underpriced, then that is an opportunity that you can take advantage of. When you use this approach, it is important that you should not be biased about anything. Always keep an open mind and do your best to understand the company before you make any real investment.

Stock split

In a 'stock split,' a stock is split, and so it gets divided. For example, if a stock or share costs $40. After a stock split, then you will end up with two stocks at $20 each. Take note that it does not always have to be an equal split. The point is that the stock will be divided, and so its price should also be divided accordingly. This is usually done by companies when the price of its shares gets too high. So, they move for a stock split to lower the price. This is also because investors tend to shy away from stocks that are too pricey. Now, this is actually a good sign. It usually means that the business is doing good. Normally, after a stock split, the price of stocks still continues to increase. When you use this strategy, you should pay attention to companies that just declared a stock split. This normally signifies that they're doing well.

Now, you should be careful. A common mistake is to fall for a reverse split. This is like a stock split, but it is not good. In a reverse split, stocks are combined, which causes the price of stocks to increase. Since there is an increase in price, it might look as if it were a good investment, although that is not really the case. Here is an example. Let us say that there are 10 stocks at $10 each. In case of a reverse split, then you will end up with five stocks at $20 each. This is the opposite of a reverse split. In this case, the price of stocks increases not because the company is doing well, but it's because of a manipulative action made by the company. Hence, do not forget that a simple increase in the price of stocks is not good enough of an indicator that the company is doing well.

Take note that, although a stock split is often a good indication that the company is doing well, you should still do your own research before you make an investment. A stock split alone is not enough. You should take a closer look at the company and study it carefully. This way you can increase the chances of making a good investment.

Stock mastery

The more that you know and understand a particular stock, the more likely that you can predict its price movement. This is the idea behind this strategy. When you use this approach, you should choose a particular stock that you like which you think is profitable. Your job is to make sure that you read and analyze the said stock every day. After some time, you will notice that since you know the said stock so well already, you can easily predict its behavior in the market, and this will allow you to take advantage of it and make a nice profit.

Read and find out as much as you can about your chosen stock. Now, it is also common that you might suddenly realize that the stock is not a profitable investment as you study it. This is well and good because it will help you lower your losses. In this case, do not be discouraged. Simply move to another stock and start over. Do not consider your efforts as a waste. If you end up with a losing stock, then be thankful for the fact that you have saved money by not making any real investment.

Once you gain mastery over a stock, then you can start taking advantage of it. But, how do you know if you have mastered a particular stock? There is no strict rule regarding this matter. The important thing is that you can predict its price movements correctly most of the time. Once you attain mastery over a particular stock, then feel free to master another stock. However, when you move to studying another stock, do not neglect the previous stock that you have already mastered. The more stocks that you get to master, the better chances you have of making a large profit. Do not rush the process of learning and researching information about a particular stock. Take note that you are aiming for mastery, and not just having mere knowledge of a stock.

Develop your own

As a professional investor, you can develop your own strategy. It can be as simple as making a few adjustments to the strategies that you already know, but you are also free to come up with an entirely new strategy of your own. The life of a full-time investor is mostly about developing a strategy. Keep in mind that the stock market is a continuously moving market. The strategy that you use should be up to date with the latest changes and developments. Therefore, as you work on your strategy, you should also keep a close eye on the stock market.

Developing your own strategy can take a long time. Be ready to go through some trial and error before you adopt a strategy and apply it using real money. This is a good time to make use of the demo account provided by your stockbroker so that you can test your strategy in a real market environment without risking any real money. If you do not want to make use of the demo account, then you can simply make small investments and see how they go.

Take note that strategies are highly sensitive. This means that even a minor change in your strategy can make a big difference. Therefore, when it comes to developing your own strategy, be sure to test it more than once even if you only have to make a small adjustment.

Chapter 3: Best Practices

Research

When it comes to choosing the right and profitable stocks to invest in, the important thing is to do your research. Remember, you should never make any investment without doing solid research. Now, it is true that many investors do their research and yet, still fail to pick the right investments. The reason why this happens is that many of these investors fail to render a sufficient amount of research.

So, just how much research is needed? There are no hard and fast rules on this matter, but you will know if it is enough once you can honestly say that you understand the stock that you intend to invest in, and that you also understand the present situation of the stock market.

This is also another reason why fundamental analysis is important. Indeed, if you are serious about doing well as an investor, then you need to do continuous research.

When you research a potential stock to invest in, you should make sure to gather quality information. Do not just limit yourself to the news, but also be open enough to consider what other investors think. There are many investors who write blog posts and articles. Although it's not required, it will also help if you take the time to consider their opinions. It is also advised that you join online groups and forums on the subject. This will not just allow you to meet people who share the same interest, but it is also a good way to learn interesting viewpoints, opportunities, and even new strategies. Again, remember to never make any investment if it is not backed up by a solid research. Otherwise, you will only end up gambling, and this is not the suggested approach since the risk of losing your investment is high if you do not conduct enough research.

Start small

It does not matter how much funds you have in your account. If you are just starting out, then it is strongly advised that you start out small. Your first objective is not to make money right away but to familiarize yourself with the trading environment. In fact, it is advised that you start out by using the demo account provided by your broker. Do not worry, once you are used to the actual market environment, and once you have a reliable strategy, then you can easily increase the amount of your investment. Again, do not rush the learning process. This can help to effectively minimize your losses.

Write a trading or investing journal

Although it's not a requirement, writing an investment journal can be very helpful, especially in the long run. You don't need to be a professional writer to come up with a journal. However, there are two things that you have to keep in mind:

- You should update your journal regularly
- You should be completely honest with everything that you write in your journal

So, what should you write in your journal? Well, you are free to write everything that is related to investing in stocks. After all, it is your journal, so feel free to do whatever you want with it. Ideally, your journal should contain your reasons for investing in stocks, your goals and objectives, the stocks that you are currently studying, lessons and mistakes, as well as your strategies, among other others.

Having a journal will allow you to view yourself from a different perspective, from a standpoint that is free from any form of bias and prejudice. As you can see, this is why it is important that you update your journal regularly and that you should be very honest.

In the first few weeks, you might not appreciate the benefits of having a journal. However, just continue writing your journal. After some time, you will start to appreciate its importance, especially once you notice your progress.

As you should already know, a journal is not just a notebook that you write in. Rather, it should serve as a mirror of yourself that will help you see your strengths and weaknesses. It will also reveal to you lessons that you would have otherwise, overlooked. Needless to say, you should read your journal from time to time. As you read, you should also make reflections. Try to learn as much as you can from your journal. Keep an open mind and be open to new ideas and realizations.

Cash out

There are investors who like to keep all their profits in their account. The reason for this is they want to increase their funds. After all, the bigger the funds, the bigger the potential profit. However, although there is nothing wrong with growing your funds, you should understand that making a withdrawal is also important. If you do not withdraw your profits, then it's no different from using a mere demo account. Also, cashing out is a simple yet effective way of minimizing your risks and losses. Take note that as long as your money is in your account, it will be continuously exposed to risks. You don't need to withdraw all of the profits when you cash out of course. If you want, you can simply withdraw just 20% of your total profits. The important thing is that you make a withdrawal and enjoy the fruits of your work.

Take a break

Although the activities of an investor can be fun, it can also be tiring, especially in the long run. Hence, do not hesitate to give yourself some time off and take a break every now and then. Now, when you take a break, do not be like other people who still worry about their investments. It is advised that you close down all your positions before you take a break. This way, you would not have to worry about anything. When you take a break, do not even think about your investments. This is the best time to relax and just have fun. Just enjoy your vacation or at least have a movie night at home. The important thing is that you relax as much as you can. Although, after taking your break, you are expected to work even harder. So, enjoy it as much as you can.

Continuous improvement

Just as the market continues to move, you should always strive for continuous improvement. Do not let this book or any other books put any limitation on you. Always do your best to improve. Even if you think that you already know enough about a particular stock, you should still try to learn more about it. There is no end to continuous improvement.

You should also expand your circle and meet other investors. This is a good way to develop your skills and learn interesting views and strategies. One way you can improve yourself is by making short-term goals. Do your best to meet these goals. For example, aiming for a small 3% gain if you are just starting out is good. You can then raise the bar as you get used to investing in the stock market.

Diversify your risks

Diversifying your risk is another strategy that you should observe. This is not new, but it is also followed in this business. You are probably familiar with the saying that you should never put all of your eggs in one basket. There is no strategy or amount of research that can guarantee the success of any investment. Of course, this does not mean that you should no longer do your research and study the market. However, you need to be ready just in case the worst happens. After all, there are so many things that can happen in the course of the investment. This is why it is important that you diversify your risks. When it comes to investing in stocks, you need to spread your investments by opening multiple positions. Do not gamble all your money in one trading position. By diversifying your risks, there is still a chance for you to end up making a profit even if you lose one of your positions. Now, a common mistake beginners make is taking some of their positions for granted. They think that since they will open multiple trades, they can still survive even if they make some bad investments. Although this may be true, it is wrong to take any position for granted. If you observe expert and successful investors, you will see just how careful they are before they enter into any position. Even though they always closely follow the market, they are very cautious about opening or closing a position. They do not allow themselves to be overcome by overconfidence. Instead, they keep up with the best practices and stick to their winning strategy. Again, learn to diversify your risks. Doing so can save you from sudden and unexpected changes in the market.

Professional approach

Most people start investing in stocks as a hobby. Although there is nothing wrong with this, it is not the suggested approach. The problem with investing in stocks as a hobby is that in the stock market, you often receive what you deserve. Hence, if you take it as a hobby, then expect to gain (or lose) something as a mere hobby. Do not expect to make continuous profits. Taking something as a mere hobby signifies lack of dedication and commitment. You can compare this with the long hours that professional investors spend studying the market, and yet they are still very careful every time that they make an investment. So, what should you do? Instead of thinking of it as a mere hobby, you should take a professional approach. If you are busy and know that you cannot give it as much time as you would, then just be a part-time trader. That way you do not have to open multiple positions regularly. The important thing is to emphasize and know that you are serious about it. Do not take it lightly but give it as much commitment, time, and effort as it deserves.

Chapter 4: Mistakes to Avoid

Chasing after your losses

In gambling, gamblers are often advised not to chase after their losses. However, the surprising truth is that even those who are well aware of this advice still continue to chase after their losses. How does this happen? Well, you need to understand how this works. So, what does it mean to chase after your losses? This normally happens after you experience a bad loss. We all have the tendency or desire to recover our losses. Since you have already given it time and effort, you still want to make a profit even if it's just small. However, to do this, you will usually have to invest a bigger amount of funds. This is where the problem comes in. The amount that you invest may be difficult for your total finances to handle. Again, remember that there is no amount of preparation that can guarantee the positive outcome of any investment. The problem here is, if you lose that position, then you will certainly end up with a loss so huge that there may not be any practical way to get back your losses.

So, what should you do? Instead of chasing after your losses, experts advise that you should chase after more profits. After all, in the course of your investing career, it is unavoidable that you will encounter a number of losing positions every now and then. This is normal. The important thing is that you make a profit once you combine everything. Chasing after your losses forces you to take an aggressive strategy, which is often not good. Although chasing your losses do not always end up in a negative outcome, it is just too risky. If you continue to chase your losses, then you will most probably end up losing more money in the long run because of its high-risk nature.

Using an untested strategy

This is a common, yet serious mistake committed by beginners. You should keep in mind that even minor changes in a strategy can have a strong overall impact on the effectiveness of the strategy. Remember, you should never use an untested strategy. Be sure to run multiple trials before you use it to make a real investment. A good way to do this is to take advantage of the demo account provided by your online stock broker. Now, it is unavoidable that you will soon have to make changes or slight adjustments to your strategy. Remember, for every adjustment that you make, be sure to run some trials before you use it with real money. It is easy to get lazy and be tempted to skip the testing stage, but that is a serious error. You should get used to testing your strategy, as it will be a normal part of your life as a trader as you continue to develop your winning strategy.

Relying completely on expert advice

As a beginner, there is nothing wrong with listening to the advice given by so-called 'experts.' Most beginners even have their favorite blogs that they visit every now and then. However, it should be noted that it is wrong to completely rely on the pieces of advice given by these 'experts.' The sad truth is that many of these so-called 'experts' are not even real experts. In today's world, it is fairly easy to make anyone look like an expert, especially when you harness the power of social media.

Since many of these 'experts' are not even real experts, relying on their advice can be a serious problem. You should also consider that even the real experts out there still commit mistakes from time to time. If you are serious about becoming a professional investor, then you need to develop your own understanding and view of the stock market.

Of course, you are free and even encouraged to listen to the views and pieces of advice given by other stock investors, but you should only treat them as they are: a mere advice or suggestion. You still hold the final say and have total control over your own investments. Even as a beginner, you should aim to develop your own understanding of the market. Otherwise, you might end up being controlled by others, and this is not good for you and your investments. Feel free to listen to others but always take their words and ideas with a grain of salt. Remember, in this line of business you are your own boss.

Taking weak trading positions

Another common pitfall to avoid is having weak positions. Sadly, many investors end up with weak investments or positions that will most likely result in a loss. This normally happens because they make investments even if they are not sure of their positions. Just because you have spent hours of serious research does not mean that you are now in the position to make a wise investment decision. As a professional investor, it should be considered normal for you to spend hours doing research and analysis of the different stocks in the market. Now, before you make any investment, you should ensure that your decisions are backed up by solid research. If you honestly do not feel confident about a certain investment, then do not make any investment. You are not obliged to enter any position, especially if you are not feeling uneasy about it. Instead of keeping weak positions, it is better for you not to keep any investment at all.

Being a victim of the 'pump and dump' scheme

This is another pitfall that beginners fall into. To understand how it works, you should know what a 'pump and dump' scheme is. It is a fraudulent scheme. In a pump and dump scheme, the people behind it pump a particular stock by using promotional hype. It will appear as if a certain stock is a good investment. In today's world, it is very easy to promote and share information via the Internet. Once people believe that a particular stock is a good investment, they put money into it. Now, this will make the price of the said stock increase. This is the pumping stage. As the price increases, the more it will convince other investors to make an investment.

This is where the trick comes in. Once the price of the stock reaches a certain amount or when the people recognize that it is already overpriced for its real value, then the ones behind the scheme make a sell order. As a result, the fraudsters make a profit by selling it at a higher price. This is the dumping stage. Now, the drawback here is that its price will now fall, and those who are holding on to these stocks will end up with stocks that have a steadily declining price.

This is another reason why it is important for you to have your own understanding of the stock market. If you just listen to what other people tell you, then you will most likely end up as a victim of the pump and dump scheme. Yes, this fraudulent scheme happens in the real stock market, so you should be aware and exercise caution in your dealings.

Trading aggressively

Another mistake to avoid is being too aggressive. Now, being too aggressive might yield a higher profit, but it is also a quick way to lose your money. It is quite tempting to take the aggressive approach because it offers a higher return but it is also very risky to the point that if you keep on following this approach, then there is a good chance that you will soon lose your money. If you are just starting out, it is strongly advised that you stay away from any aggressive strategies. Or, if you have to be aggressive in any way, then be sure to control it and minimize the aggressiveness. Instead, you should focus on increasing your rate of success. You can do this by developing your winning strategy.

Learn to minimize your losses by minimizing your risks. Make sure that every trading position you enter is one you studied well and is backed up by research. Be conservative as possible. This does not mean that you should no longer focus on making a profit, you just have to avoid taking an extreme measure to gain a significant profit. Keep in mind that there is no end to investing, so you do not have to hurry. The stock market is always open, and it will continue to function no matter what. So, do not be impatient. Instead, keep an eye on available opportunities and be sure to grab them when they present themselves. Instead of focusing too much on the money that you want to make, focus on increasing your rate of success by always studying the stock market.

Conclusion

Thanks for making it through to the end of this book. We hope it was informative and that it provided you with all of the tools you need to achieve your goals whatever they may be.

The next step is to apply everything that you have learned. Investing in the stock market can be an interesting journey. Be ready to face some challenges along the way. The important thing is to keep on learning. Take note that to learn the strategies in this book, you have to practice them. Investing in stocks is just like learning a new skill. It does take some time and effort, but it is very much worth it. Again, do not rush the development process. The more that you learn, the more that you can minimize your losses and increase your profits.

If you want to achieve financial freedom or simply want to increase your income, then this book is for you. Investing in stocks can be challenging, but it is full of rewards for those who take the time and effort to learn it. There are people out there who earn their full-time income simply by investing in stocks. If you want a successful life by being your own boss, then give this wonderful opportunity a try.

Feel free to review this book and make your own reflections and modifications. Remember, you are dealing with a live and continuously moving market, so it is only right that you always strive for continuous improvement. This book has given you the tools to achieve total financial freedom. It is up to you to turn your newfound knowledge into actual practice. Finally, if you found this book useful in any way, a review on Amazon is always appreciated!

Rental Property Investing

How to Create Wealth and Passive Income Through Intelligent Real Estate Investing

Table of Contents

Introduction
Chapter 1: Why Rental Properties?
Chapter 2: Location Matters
Chapter 3: Which Properties Make the Best Rentals?
Chapter 4: Important Factors When Choosing a Property
Chapter 5: Your Team
Chapter 6: Making an Offer
Chapter 7: Negotiation
Chapter 8: Financing
Chapter 9: What Are the Risks Involved?
Chapter 10: How to Manage Your Properties
Chapter 11: How to Know When to Exit
Conclusion

© Copyright 2018 by _____ - All rights reserved.

The following eBook is reproduced below with the goal of providing information that is as accurate and reliable as possible. Regardless, purchasing this eBook can be seen as consent to the fact that both the publisher and the author of this book are in no way experts on the topics discussed within and that any recommendations or suggestions that are made herein are for entertainment purposes only. Professionals should be consulted as needed prior to undertaking any of the action endorsed herein.

This declaration is deemed fair and valid by both the American Bar Association and the Committee of Publishers Association and is legally binding throughout the United States.

Furthermore, the transmission, duplication or reproduction of any of the following work including specific information will be considered an illegal act irrespective of if it is done electronically or in print. This extends to creating a secondary or tertiary copy of the work or a recorded copy and is only allowed with an expressed written consent from the Publisher. All additional rights reserved.

The information in the following pages is broadly considered to be truthful and accurate account of facts, and as such any inattention, use or misuse of the information in question by the reader will render any resulting actions solely under their purview. There are no scenarios in which the publisher or the original author of this work can be in any fashion deemed liable for any hardship or damages that may befall them after undertaking information described herein.

Additionally, the information in the following pages is intended only for informational purposes and should thus be thought of as universal. As befitting its nature, it is presented without assurance regarding its prolonged validity or interim quality. Trademarks that are mentioned are done without written consent and can in no way be considered an endorsement from the trademark holder.

Introduction

Congratulations on downloading *Rental Property Investing: How to Create Wealth and Passive Income Through Intelligent Real Estate Investing* and thank you for doing so.

The following chapters will discuss everything that you could possibly want to know about investing in properties, specifically rental properties. It can seem overwhelming and as if it's only for someone with a Master's degree in business. But real estate investing is actually much simpler than you realize! It certainly helps to have the right team on your side, especially when you're not exactly sure what you're doing. Everything from an attorney to a property manager can make the process much easier and help you to earn the highest possible profit. Basically, having the right team means the difference between failing and succeeding. You'll learn why exactly rentals make the best investments, which property types are best for renting out, and why location matters so much. Your success relies on having tenants, so you need to consider what those tenants are looking for and how to provide it to them. Different properties do well in different types of locations; a multi-family home might not do as well in the city as it would in the suburbs. And while looking at potential properties can be fun, it's the business side of things that makes it a little difficult. This book helps talk you through everything necessary to help you succeed, and teaches you how to negotiate and what to do when you're ready to make an offer. And not just that, but you'll even learn about financing, and which types of loans are the best fit for you and your business. Each financing option has different pros and cons, and you'll need to figure out which one you'd prefer. And this book doesn't just talk about the benefits, but also things that could be considered negative. You'll learn about all the risks involved when investing in a rental property, and how you know when the best time to sell is. There are some really amazing tips and tricks in this book, and you'll learn so much!

There are plenty of books on this subject on the market, thanks again for choosing this one! Every effort was made to ensure it is full of as much useful information as possible. Please enjoy!

Chapter 1: Why Rental Properties?

Property investing can be confusing, expensive, and a lot of work. One of the most confusing things is that there are many different types of properties, so most people don't even know which property brings about the best profit and opportunities. Rental properties make for great investments, especially if you're a beginner.

One of the biggest reasons is that they have a lot of different finance options. You'll more than likely need to get a loan to acquire the property, and that in itself can be difficult. There is actually a loan called the "conventional loan," which is the most sought-after type of loan for rentals. As the borrower, you are required to make a down payment of around 20 to 30 percent of the full amount you take out. And that can be a lot of money upfront, but it's actually better for you in the long run. This specific type of loan has a steady and low-interest rate, which is fantastic news for a person investing in rental properties. Think about how long you'll have the property for. Typically, it's something you'd like for decades because there will always be people needing to rent, and the normal duration of a loan is around 15 to 30 years. So, having that low steady interest rate over the span of 30 years is the best possible outcome. You don't want to end up paying double the loan back, which is what can happen if your interest rate is too high. Also, a conventional loan will use your rental property as security and collateral for your loan. That means you don't have to put up your own house or car as security, which will be good if for some reason the property doesn't work out. And as an added bonus, the income you would potentially make from your rental isn't calculated into the loan. Meaning that the income you can expect to receive from your rental doesn't come into play on whether you get accepted for the loan or not. However, it's important to take the expected income into consideration so that you know whether you'd make enough to pay back the loan in time. If your income ends up being too little, you'll have to use other means of money to pay the loan back. You'll end up losing money over time! Make sure to calculate your potential income when deciding how much to pay back the loan each month. If a conventional loan doesn't sound like the right fit for you, you can also try a private funding loan. The negative of this type of loan is that it has a higher interest rate. On the flip side, it takes a much shorter amount of time to get this type of loan than a conventional one. Choose a private funding loan if you know that your rental investment has a really good chance of succeeding; if you have a great business plan and know the location, property, and everything else adds up perfectly for success. If you'd prefer a conventional loan, but like the quickness of a private funding loan, then you could actually get a private funding loan for a short-term need until your other conventional loan is accepted.

Rental properties have a lot of flexibility, which is another great reason to choose them! It ends up being left up to you on how you'd like to rent out your property, all while making a profit. You choose what works best for you and how to implement it. Think about it this way. There are long term and short-term type rentals. Both have negative and positive reasons to choose them, and it's up to you on what works best for you. There are the more traditional long-term rentals, which typically have a lease term of 6 to 12 months. This ensures that you are guaranteed tenants and a steady rate of occupancy, which could last for decades depending on how long the tenants would like to stay and whether they're actually good tenants. Then there are the short-term rentals, similar to how Airbnb is run. These have at most a lease term of 6 months, usually much shorter than that. They can be a little more difficult to keep up with, and you run the risk of putting up with not so great tenants. However, because it's such a short time of leasing, you're able to charge a higher income and make a bigger profit. One big benefit of having a rental property is the option of actually living there yourself. You can live in your own property, and rent out all the other space. That means instead of you paying rent, mortgage, etc., in your own house, you can make the money to pay all that through the tenants. This works best in a house or apartment that is at least 3 bedrooms and has at least 2 bathrooms. You can take up one of the bedrooms/bathrooms, and rent out the others. And it's up to you which rooms you rent out. You can decide to either take the master bedroom and rent out the smaller rooms, or take a small room and rent out the master for more money. Doing this also has the added bonus of a more convenient financing options since it's easier to finance your main home residence.

Rental property investing is a very low risk, which is why it's such a good choice for beginners. You can learn all you need to know about the process of investing in rentals, and either keep up with them or move on to bigger properties. You go through the entire process of buying a rental, looking it over, adding up the various expenses, and learning how to manage it, all without worrying about a high risk. Of course, as a beginner, you'll definitely make mistakes and deal with many issues. But since rental properties tend to have a slightly higher turn around rate, you'll be able to learn from those mistakes and fix them for the future. You'll only make a mistake once, so eventually, you reach that optimal level of success. Plus, doing all the work yourself means you'll be able to understand what goes into managing a property. Which means, at the point when you're financially able to hire someone to manage it for you, you'll still be able to understand what's going on in your property and won't be taken advantage of.

When making investments, thinking about the long run is always a good idea. You want something that will last for a very long time, and bring in a steady income. Something that can keep bringing in money even past the typical "retirement" age. And that's where rental properties come in. They have the most to offer in the tumultuous world of real estate. They have a big enough profit that all the costs you've made for the investment are covered, and they bring in an income and a good investment return that lasts many years. Long enough, in fact, that you can pay off the loan and make a profit. You even have the option to sell eventually, getting all your money back plus extra. It means being patient of course. This isn't the type of investment that will earn you quick money. But you'll be earning a great income if you can think in the long term. And not just a normal income, but passive income which is the best type. You can go about your life, doing other work if you want, all while earning profit. A rental doesn't take up too much of your time, so having just one or two can be a great way to earn some passive income with it not taking up too much of your time.

Chapter 2: Location Matters

Location is probably the most important thing when figuring out which property you'd like to invest in. After all, your future tenants will want an area that best suits their needs, and one they can call home for many years to come. That means that not only do you need to check out the property and its neighbors, but also the surrounding area. How many grocery stores there are, whether it's walkable or not, nearby gas stations, what kind of restaurants are around it, etc. You have to think about who you want to rent to and find the best location that caters to that type of person. If you'd prefer renting to young professionals, then a city-type area with hip restaurants, local attractions, and organic grocery stores makes more sense than an area in the suburbs with a lot of kid-friendly attractions. The reverse is true as well; if you know your tenants will most like be families, then choosing a property in a good school district makes more sense than one being next door to a hip bar. And it's not just the local attractions that you have to consider. Think about where exactly your property is sitting. Is it on a spacious street with good lighting and lots of street parking, or is the only entrance down a dark alley? Families prefer good yards and lots of safe outdoor space, so a multi-family home on a cul-de-sac will rent much better than one on a busy street. You might be able to find a great fixer-upper for pretty cheap, but if no one rents it because of the location, then it'll end up just costing you much more than you'd want.

Keep in mind that location is really the only permanent thing about your property. You can change the wall colors, change the furniture, even rebuild completely! But you're always going to be in that specific location, so make sure it's one that you'd like to stay with for many years to come. In fact, keep an eye out on future trends and up and coming neighborhoods. If you know that a neighborhood is not so great now, but there are plans to rebuild and revitalize it in the next few years, you could buy a property there for very cheap and fix it up. Once you're ready to rent it out, the neighborhood will be much better, and people will be more willing to live in a cool and hip area. This will also help a lot if you end up selling. You could potentially make a very good profit! Just be careful because there could be ideas thrown around to fix the neighborhood up, but nothing actually happens. Look around at what other kinds of businesses there are, and if there are condos and cafes popping up.

Where the property is geographically located is pretty important. There's such a thing as supply and demand, even in real estate. It's best to look around the area and see how many properties there are for rent. You don't want to be number 40 on a very long list; that's just too many, and the area is saturated with available properties. The fact that there's so many is a big indication that something's wrong with the neighborhood. Maybe the crime rate is high, or it floods every time it rains. Whatever the reason, if potential tenants see so many properties available, they'll think something is wrong and look elsewhere. You also need to look in an area that actually has a lot of people in it. If you think the idea of investing in a property in a small town is "quaint," think again! You should be in a location that actually has a good supply; supply being possible tenants. It's best to find a happy medium. Look for properties in an area that has a few for rent, but not too many, with many people for lots of options.

Location also matters when you consider who exactly you're renting to. You obviously want a location that has access to great amenities like internet, etc., but what about public transportation? Many people who live in a city don't have a car or only use their car very rarely. So, a property that has easy access to the local bus route or train will be in higher demand than one that requires a long walk just to get to the bus. What kind of amenities that are around your property depends on whether you're looking to rent to long term or short-term tenants. Those looking to stay for a long time would prefer to be close to schools, hospitals, grocery stores, etc. However, short-term tenants, like Airbnb guests, typically prefer the more touristy stuff. They would need good access to public transportation, restaurants, and easy access to activities. While garage parking would be important for long-term rentals, short-term tenants probably wouldn't care as much. The first thing to do is figure out who you'd rather rent to, and choose the best location off that. Remember though that both long and short-term tenants want to be in safe areas with good utilities.

Speaking more about short-term tenants, keep in mind that you might not be able to do traditional rentals. A multi-family house in the suburbs would be great for long-term tenants, but most Airbnb guests would prefer to stay closer to the city. They would be fine with smaller rooms and not every amenity (depending on the length of stay). Many tourists visit to see the city and all it has to offer, so they're more willing to overlook things that long-term tenants would prefer to have in their house.

Location is also important to how much of a profit you'll make. Different areas mean different costs, and what you could charge for rent in one location could be way too expensive for another. Research other properties in the area, similar to the one you're looking to invest in. See how much they're costing, and how much other property holders are charging. It's important to also keep track of how much it will cost you every month to run the property. Some months will be cheaper than others, but sometimes you'll have something unexpected come up. You don't need to replace the water heater every year, but adding it to your expenses will help you to know how much exactly your property will cost you over the years. A property that looks amazing has all the latest upgrades, and a beautiful yard will rent much better in an area with other similar properties. On the flip side, if you have an older property that is livable but runs down, you'll only be able to charge so much for it. Especially in an area that has very beautiful and modern homes. If the upgraded home next door rents for $1400 a month, and your property is about worth half that, then you'd only be able to charge your tenants $700 a month. Which is good news for them, but you'll end up paying a lot out of pocket. Whereas if the older property is in a neighborhood with other older homes, and the one next door is $1400, then you'd be able to charge the same amount.

You really have to think about location long-term when investing in rental properties. And not just about the property, but the land itself. If you choose one that is in a very good location, with high demand, then you can make a very good profit down the road. This is known as real estate appreciation, and it considers how valuable land is, and how much more valuable it will be in the future. If there is a neighborhood being built by a lot of empty land, then it's pretty much guaranteed that the land next to it will also have homes in the next few years. If you invest in one of those first homes, before the area really starts to boom, then you'll be able to make a great profit later on down the road. Once a neighborhood is built, people will want amenities. Which means restaurants, grocery stores, malls, and movie theaters. And once those are built, many more people will want to move to the area. By buying ahead of the curve, you'll already have real estate available for those looking to rent. You'll be able to up the rental rate once more things become available around your property, which means you'll be making a bigger profit. And eventually, you can even sell if you'd prefer. What about a location that's next to many businesses? Maybe you've stumbled on a home for sale in an area where new restaurants, pharmacies, and stores are popping up. If you invest in the right property, the land might end up being worth more than the house. You can rent out the property for as long as you'd like, and sell once you've been approached by a big business.

Another thing to consider when looking at locations are the local laws. Eviction laws can be a pain and end up having a negative effect on you and your property. Obviously, you don't want to actually go through the process of evicting someone, but sometimes it's a necessary evil. If you have a tenant not paying rent, then the legal thing to do is evict them. However, in some states, it can actually take months to legally evict a person, which means they can technically stay on your property and not pay. You end up losing months of money waiting around for the law. And what about changing the rent? Sometimes the property value goes up, and your rent needs to keep up with the area. However, some places have what is called rent stabilization laws, which means you might not be able to actually raise the rent however you like. And what about their security deposit? Most tenants take pretty good care of the property they're renting, but sometimes you end up with ones that trash your place. Or even accidentally damage something. That's where their security deposit comes in. Typically, you use that to pay for whatever damage they inflict, accidentally or otherwise. But if it comes into question, some states will side with the tenant no matter what. It's best to find out which areas are the most landlord friendly, and figure out a location based on that.

Chapter 3: Which Properties Make the Best Rentals?

We all know that mistakes happen; accidentally saying the wrong thing, bumping into someone, or dropping what you were just holding. But while these mistakes are pretty small and can be overlooked, choosing the wrong rental property can really mess up your new real estate company. It can mean a lot of unnecessary stress, be very expensive to fix, and even cause you yourself to feel ill. So how do you make sure to choose the best property? There's so many out there, and there's a lot of different questions you can ask yourself to help.

What to buy, what to not buy, how many bedrooms, should the property have a garage, what are the neighbors like, what's the color of the property, how old is it, how big is it. Keeping these basic questions in mind will help you to find the best property for your business.

Multi-Family Homes: The ultimate goal is to find long-term tenants, which is hard to do with single family homes, depending on the family. When there are only one or two bedrooms, tenants might stay for a year or two but eventually move out. Think about it - people usually end up getting married and having kids and need a lot of space for their future plans. By choosing three or four-bedroom houses for your rentals, you're ensuring that your tenants will stay for at least 5 years! And if you ever get to the point of needing to sell, three to four-bedroom houses sell best because, again, of all those families looking for the perfect home.

Single-Family Homes: These homes probably make the next best rentals. They're the easiest to manage, mainly because those renting them tend to treat these types of houses as if they are their own homes. While some people like living in apartments, most would prefer a house with a yard. However, most people also don't want too big of a house or to buy a house outright, which is why they're renting. It's possible for you to find tenants that would prefer to stay renting a single-family home for decades, which would definitely benefit you. Since the renters see the home as theirs, they also usually do some of the repairs needed and take better care of the yard. And unlike apartments, in single-family homes, the tenant pays all of the utilities, which makes it much easier for you.

Apartment: Two-bedroom apartments are actually pretty good, and liked by a lot of people. People seem to be moving slightly away from the suburban life, and wanting to live closer to the city. It can be difficult for families because it's hard to find a two or three-bedroom house in a city. So many families compromise and look for a two-bedroom apartment. The type of person can affect your rental business too; you want to rent to a professional, someone you know that will be able to afford your rent. And typically, a professional single person prefers a two-bedroom apartment over a studio or one bedroom. It's extra space for their office or a work out room. Studios and one-bedroom apartments usually have a high turnover in their tenants, even with a 12-month contract. So, renting out a two-bedroom apartment is a good middle ground for someone looking to rent a place for a few years. You can try investing in and renting out a one bedroom or studio apartments, but you run the risk of a high turnover rate. Of course, it's possible to find a single person that is professional and wants to stay in the apartment long term, but the norm is typically the opposite. If you're looking for the best possible chance to make a profit with an apartment, then a two bedroom makes the most sense.

Chapter 4: Important Factors When Choosing a Property

Just like there are types of properties that make for fantastic rentals, there are ones that really aren't great and tend to cost you more in the long run. You really don't want to be putting in more money than you're making; eventually, you'll either lose a bunch of money or go out of business, and both of those scenarios are terrible ones! There are several things you can consider when choosing the right property, and several things to keep an eye out for that you'll know to stay away from. Of course, an important thing to remember are the different trends and fads in your current location. While choosing to invest in a studio apartment might seem like not a great idea, if your location is primarily in a city then having a few smaller apartments to rent out would make sense. Here's a list of things to consider when looking for ideal properties:

Bedrooms: Bedrooms are always top of the list when looking at properties. The number of bedrooms caters to different types of tenants, and it all depends on who you'd like to rent to. You also have to think of whether you'd like to sell or not. Studio and one-bedroom apartments usually have a higher turn around rental time, so if you're looking for long term tenants then stay away from those type of properties. Sometimes more bedrooms can cause issues too. If you have too many rooms, then typically your tenants will be ones with a lot of children. Which isn't necessarily a bad thing, but kids can cause a lot of wear and tear to a property. You have to think about how kids can break, tear, and stain, and decide whether it's worth it. If you do try renting out a house with many bedrooms, make sure you have an iron-clad security deposit!

Age: Older homes can be a lot more expensive to fix. You can probably buy one for pretty cheap, which is great, but you also have to think about how much it'll cost to actually fix it. You could end up spending more in the long run on an older home than the upfront costs of a newer one. A simple project could end up being a lot more hassle than originally thought, and it's entirely possible that the previous work done on it over the years wasn't up to standard and code. Energy costs will be higher in an older property as well. You can get around that by having the tenants pay their own utility bills, but if they actually figure it out, then you'll end up having a higher turnover rate in renters. To bypass all this stress, you could simply just invest in newer homes.

Garage: Homes without a garage don't usually stay rented for long periods of times. Think about where you're located and what the weather is like. Does it rain or snow a lot? Weather can cause a lot of wear and tear to a person's car, and end up costing the tenant money. Even hot days can make it unbearable, especially if your tenant has leather seats! Plus, having lots of storage is really nice. If you're investing in single family homes, there might not be a lot of storage. So, having a garage can really help sell your property. If you're looking for long-term tenants, then it's best to stay away from homes without garages.

Utilities: While most renters don't like paying for utilities separate from their rent, it's actually an ideal situation for you. Having the tenants pay their own utility bills is definitely a better situation to be in for you. Think about it like this - if your tenant doesn't have to worry about utilities, they'll probably leave the AC running all the time, especially during summer. Maybe there's a small drip in the faucet; they don't mention it because they're not paying for it, and it ends up costing an extra few hundred dollars a year. So, it's definitely recommended to stay away from properties that have all the bills being paid for by you the owner. That can be a little more difficult in multi-family homes, so try to find ones that at least have electricity and heat being paid for by the renter. It's possible to have them pay the water as well, through a system called master metered. Your renters are able to pay their own water bill through it, which will help you immensely.

Lawn: Stay away from properties with large yards! Tenants won't expect to take care of the yard of a property they're renting, which means it'll be up to you. So, either you'll have to spend your own time and money keeping up with the yard, hire someone to do it which will cost money, or make the tenant do it which they won't be too happy about. On the flip side, if you're renting out a multi-family home, it's important for most families to have a yard that their kids can run around in. Many people like having a space for recreation, planting, or backyard bar-b-que's, so your best option is finding homes that have yards but in a smaller scale. Keep in mind other outdoor features too. Do you really want to deal with the upkeep of a fountain? What about a pool in the backyard? Pool maintenance can be difficult and expensive, and it will most likely be up to you as the landlord to keep up with. If something breaks or malfunctions, the tenant will expect you to fix it in a timely manner. Instead of all that stress and hassle, invest in properties that don't even have all that extra stuff.

Parking: Tenants love a good parking spot! Some places have enough room for just one vehicle, which will deter most people. Even if you're renting to only one person, they could have visitors over who then wouldn't have anywhere to park. Parking off the street is something most tenants prefer as well, so stay away from properties that don't have adequate parking. Look for covered or garages, and try to find more than one parking spot.

Location: Location is probably one of the most important factors when looking at a property. People want to live in an area they love, and one that they'll want to actually be in. They'll want to visit local restaurants, walk around, be by their favorite grocery store. If they have children, they'll want to be in the right school district or close to a good daycare. And for many people, a shorter commute is definitely ideal. Of course, tenants will want to be in a safe neighborhood as well, so it's best to look for properties in an area with a low crime rate. If you're in the middle of the city with lots of cafes, restaurants, and boutiques, then it makes sense to look for properties that cater to a more "hip" crowd. Most families tend to be in actual neighborhoods or suburbs, so investing in a large multi-family home in the middle of a city doesn't really make sense. The opposite of that also applies. If you're looking to invest in properties in more of a suburb-like setting, then choosing a studio or one-bedroom apartments wouldn't be a good financial decision.

Number of Tenants: How many tenants you'd like to rent to will definitely factor into the properties you're looking at. Typically, it's one person to a bedroom unless your tenants are a couple. There are a few exceptions though. If you're looking near a college, it might make sense to invest in a large house with many bedrooms. More than five if you can wing it! Doing it this way means that instead of renting to one or two students, you would be able to rent out the home to multiple students. Of course, keep in mind that the more tenants than, the more wear and tear you'll have on the property. But this is where location comes into play. By investing in a multi-family home near a college, you're ensured that there will always be students looking for a place to rent. The turn-over might be high; most students graduate within four years. But the college will always be there, so there will always be students. If you'd only like to have just a few tenants, then it makes more sense to go after the smaller properties. Renting out a 5-bedroom house to only 2 people can mean that you lose money on maintenance and utility costs. It's a large space, one that would need expensive fixing up if something happens, and having the rent of just two tenants probably wouldn't cover the issue.

Chapter 5: Your Team

There's a lot that goes into investing in real estate, especially rental properties. You can try to take on everything, but you'll find yourself getting overwhelmed pretty quickly. Things will be much easier if you build a team, one that you can rely on for many years to come. It's possible if you're buying just one small property, then you could potentially do everything yourself. But honestly, that sounds like bankruptcy just waiting to happen! Because it's not just a property manager that would be helpful, but someone to take care of all the legalities and information you just don't know much about.

Real Estate Agent: A real estate agent is going to become your best friend. You'll need someone that knows all about short sales, foreclosures, and how to broker. Because chances are that those are the types of properties, you'll end up investing in.

Accountant: You'll want to make sure your business is set up legally, and that's something an accountant can help with. You also don't want to have to worry about taxes and everything that goes into it. Not only can taxes be confusing for a business, but if you mess up then you might get audited by the IRS and possible owe a lot of money.

Attorney: Another person you absolutely need to have on your team is an attorney. They can help with all the necessary paperwork and contracts, which you'll be writing a lot of. You'll need contracts between you and the tenants, between you and your loan people, and between you and anyone else you end up working with. One small mistake in a contract can mean you end up losing money and possibly even your property. Contracts are also very important if you end up being taken to court. Let's say you have a contract between you and your tenant. You put in there that it's a 12-month contract, which means after 12 months everything in there needs to be renegotiated, including the rent payment. During the 12 months you have in there that the rent stays as is, but once the lease term is up, then you can raise the rent due to property taxes, etc. So, in the new contract, you put in there that rent has been raised by just $20, which the tenant agrees to. They sign the contract, and now have the obligation to pay their original rent, plus $20. But instead of doing that, they keep paying what they originally paid. You're owed that money, but you're not getting it. Because of them signing the contract, you're able to take them to court (if necessary), and they're legally required to pay you what you're owed. If you didn't have that contract, then you never would've been paid that money. An attorney can help make sure your contracts are worded in your favor and with any court proceedings if you need them.

Property Inspector: You need to know the condition of the home you're interested in investing in, whether it's a good deal or just not worth it. A good property inspector can help you to understand everything that's needed to make the potential home worth renting out. The property could look perfectly fine, but an inspector does more than just look at the cosmetic value. They look into the wiring, plumbing, the roof condition, the condition of the insulation, and even the structural integrity. They look over everything and helps you to know exactly how much of an investment you'd need to make. Having one on your team is definitely a benefit to you and to them. You can keep using the same inspector for each property, especially if you know they're very thorough and take their job seriously. If you're insistent on buying a property that might have some big money issues, your inspector can tell you exactly how much it would cost to fix them. You can then take that number to the sellers and renegotiate the selling price. A property inspector can actually save you a lot of money and hassle in the long run.

Mortgage Lender: You really want a great mortgage lender on your team. Someone who asks you questions knows their industry and provides you with several options to meet your specific needs. It's up to you to be responsible for each document you're signing and having a mortgage lender who actually takes the time to explain them to you will definitely benefit you. They can help you with any issues that come up and work with you if anything happens to your current mortgage program. You need one who stays in touch and makes sure that you close on your loan in a timely manner. It's entirely possible to end up losing a lot of money because of a bad mortgage lender, so make sure you find one that is really good.

Estate Attorney: Different from a real estate attorney, an estate attorney is someone who helps you specifically and not your business. They can still give you great advice, but they are there to help draft your will and plan what happens to your estate once you're gone. It can be a difficult thing to think about at the best of times, but it's especially difficult if you have a lot of properties. What happens to those properties once you move on? Who do they go to? You need to decide if they are getting passed on to a specific family member or just leave them for the bank. Keep in mind that it's not just you that you need to think of though. You probably have a lot of tenants, who rely on you for their housing needs. So, once you're gone and the properties are no longer in your control, what happens to them? That's where an estate attorney comes in. You can work together to draft a will that takes care of all your tenants, and whether they can stay at your properties for a certain amount of time, etc. You definitely don't want everyone evicted just because you're no longer around!

Property Manager: You might start out with just one or two properties, and be able to handle it all on your own. But at some point, you'll start becoming overwhelmed and not sure how to handle everything thrown at you. And that's when you bring in a property manager. It's all in the name - they are someone who is there specifically to manage your properties, so you don't have to. They deal with all the little issues that pop up, things that you really shouldn't have to figure out yourself. Maybe one of the tenants is blaring music at 3 in the morning. Is that something you really want to deal with? Instead, unleash your property manager and let them handle it! And while they're technically your employee and you're paying them to do all this, they also need to be someone you can work closely with and trust implicitly.

The Rest: There's a ton of others that you can have on your team, but many are optional and completely up to you. If your properties have a yard, then you'll need a good landscaping company. Maybe you hire someone to come in and clean once a week; obviously not the tenants living quarters, but the hallways and entrance. You could even hire someone to decorate for you, which would make the property a lot more appealing to potential renters.

Whoever you have on your team, and whether it ends up being just one person or ten, they need to be people you can really put your trust in. People who you know will help you succeed, and people you can keep on your team for many years to come. Having the right team makes all the difference when it comes to failing or succeeding, and they will help you to become the best you can be in your business.

Chapter 6: Making an Offer

Making an offer can seem like a scary thing. You've come up with a realistic price for your budget, you've considered whether it's a seller's or buyer's market, and you've done all the research needed. All that's left is to send the offer over, but that in itself can be difficult. Once you've put the offer in then, you're legally obligated to follow through. Just knowing that can make you feel nervous or unsure if you're making the right decision and whether it's one you're ok to see through. Luckily, having a real estate agent can help with the fine print. They know what to put in an official offer to make sure you, as the buyer, are protected. A basic offer is one that says you're willing to buy the property at this price, but only if the loan and conditions you prefer are met. However, it's not just the one clause that can help you, but a few other things you need to take into consideration.

View the Interior: It's important to look at the inside of the property you want to invest in. You have to know what you're getting into, and the only way to do that is by actually looking at the interior of the property. Some sellers might be finicky about it, so make sure to actually put in your offer clause that the offer is only viable if you're satisfied and approve of all the interiors in the property. The first inspection is probably the most important thing to do, before anything else just in case if you don't actually like the property and decide to not invest in it.

Numbers: It's very important that all the numbers add up before making an offer. And not just the final price of everything added up, but all the itemized things too. Look at all the statements involving income and expenses, and see if everything adds up to the expected price. For example, if the expense statement includes material costs because the owner happens to be doing the repairs himself, then renegotiate. It's not on you to pay for his repairs unless it's something you're willing to compromise on.

Taxes: Look at the tax information on the property, and make sure what the seller has been reporting adds up. You should be looking at the past few years to ensure a thorough investigation. Maybe the rent income has been pretty steady over the years but recently has become a lot higher. It's possible that's just to try and sell the property at a higher rate. By looking at the previous statements, you can see for yourself if the value is correct or not. Looking at the previous tax statements are good in general, just to make sure that the numbers are lining up.

Hiring a real estate broker to help you negotiate the offer can be very helpful and will greatly benefit you. You can try to do it yourself of course, but having that extra help is nice, and they might catch things that you don't.

Chapter 7: Negotiation

Negotiation will become your best friend. It's something you should learn inside and out because everything is negotiable, especially in real estate. There are so many things you can negotiate on - the final price of the property you're interested in, what conditions you want for the payment, how long of a payment period you'd like, how much you're renting it out for, even the furniture and various objects that can come with the property. You definitely want the best deal possible, once that leaves you feeling satisfied and proud of yourself when investing in a property. However, negotiation is a skill, one that you'll get better with as time goes on. You'll learn the various tips and tricks, and what works for you and what doesn't. It can be difficult when you're just starting out, but as you get more experience in real estate investing, you'll also get more experienced in negotiating. Here are some specific tricks you can keep in mind to help you be the best possible negotiator:

Finances: You definitely don't want to spend more than you can afford, and sometimes that happens when you're negotiating. Maybe you've gotten caught up in the process and excitement, and think that spending a few extra thousand won't hurt. But then you go back afterwards and realize you actually can't afford what you originally agreed to. Which means you either have to renegotiate or cancel the contract completely. This will cause you to lose money and whomever you're negotiating with probably won't work with you again. Either of these can have very negative effects on your business. The best thing to do? Figure out your finances before going into the negotiation. Look at how much cash you have available and any other means of money. Make a budget, and see how much potential spending you'd do for the property, how much money you have available at this exact moment, and how much of a profit you'd expect to make. You need to be profitable from the very first month or else your business can easily fail. Once you've put together your budget, you know the exact number you can't go over when negotiating. You're going to come across properties that you'd love to invest in but just can't quite afford yet. And while it'll be difficult, you might just have to walk away. Focus on the properties you can afford, and go back to the more expensive ones later, once you can realistically afford them.

Analyze: After figuring out the property you want to invest in, and once you're ready to move forward, the best step you can take is doing an analysis of the real estate market in the area. You need to figure out what the surrounding properties are going for or how much they've sold for in the past few weeks/months. Look at the selling prices, not the asking prices. The selling prices are a better example of what your new property is worth and how much you can realistically expect to ask for when negotiating. Keep that number in mind when going throughout the negotiating process and be firm!

Identify: You need to figure out if you're working in a buyer's or seller's market. One is obviously better for you, but you can still be successful in negotiations if you know ahead of time which market is trending at the moment. To know for sure, look at how many properties are listed in your area, how long they've been on the market, how much they're going for, the difference in listing and selling price, and the closing percentage. There's a big difference when investing in a property if it's a buyer's market. You're able to take a lot more time before you actually close on the deal, you have the opportunity to counter with a lower price than is originally asked, and you can even ask for some things that would be a lot more beneficial to you (like the owner leaving furniture, doing extra repairs, etc.). On the opposite side, however, things are a lot different when it's a seller's market. You need to act quickly, be prepared to pay a higher price than originally asked, offer conditions that are more beneficial to the previous owner, and remember to not expect a lot to come with the property. What makes things a lot more difficult is that competition is much more fierce with other buyers, so you have to act quickly and won't be able to bargain when doing negotiations.

Real Estate Agent: Although you might not want to spend the upfront costs of hiring a real estate agent, it's definitely worth it if you want the best deal possible. This is even more pertinent if you're a newbie, and don't really know what you're doing. A real estate agent can make the negotiation process run smoothly and takes over the negotiations completely. Some people tend to be more introverted too, so if you don't want to deal with negotiations or speaking to the seller directly, then a real estate agent makes sense! Plus, an agent is much less likely to make a mistake if you're just starting out. You can learn from them and once you know more, then try the negotiations yourself.

The Why: Why is the seller selling? It's best to know the reasons before negotiating because it will give you leverage going in. Maybe they just want to be closer to family, or maybe there's something seriously wrong with the property If it's the latter, then you can renegotiate the selling price to go way down, which would be in your favor. And knowing why they're selling helps you to know when to press harder in your negotiations and when to back down.

Negotiate, Negotiate, Negotiate: When investing in real estate, the key to getting the best possible deal and benefiting your business is to remember that you can negotiate everything, not just the price. You can try to negotiate the closing costs and date, the warranties, repairs, if the owner can leave any of the appliances or furniture, etc. Basically everything! It's especially helpful if the market is trending at a seller's market and you might not get the exact price you wanted. Instead, you can try for a deal that everyone's happy with by getting different types of benefits. Investing in rental property is all about the long term, so those extra benefits might end up putting a higher value on your property. If you decide to sell, you could end up getting a great little profit.

Compromise: It can be hard to compromise, especially if you've had your heart set on a certain price and if you tend to lean towards the stubborn side. You want to negotiate in a way where everyone ends up happy, not just you. Look at the surrounding homes that have sold recently, and negotiate the price to reflect that. For example, let's say a home nearby sold for $600,000, and it doesn't have any add-ons, like a pool, fireplace, etc. But the property you're looking at investing in has all that, plus more. So it's really not a smart business decision to try and buy that property for less than $600,000; there's no way the seller will want to sell it at that price or even negotiate. They'll just move on to the next buyer and pass you up. And if you've found a property that you really like, then don't pay more than you're willing to actually pay. While it's important to make sure the seller is happy, you need to compromise for yourself too. If you just can't reach a good price for both you and the seller, then remember it's ok to walk away. This isn't going to be your home, it's your business. And you need to make decisions that are good for your business and make sense specifically from an investor's viewpoint.

Chapter 8: Financing

Unless you have tons of extra cash laying around, you're going to need some financial help when investing in properties. It can seem overwhelming and difficult, especially if you've never gotten financing help before. As long as you have fairly good credit and a decent income, then you shouldn't have any issues borrowing money from lenders. You have a few different options to choose from:

Owner Occupant (OO): This one has very specific terms that you need to follow, but it can actually be the best option. Basically, you choose the property you'd like to buy as your rental. But instead of buying it as a business, you purchase it as a personal residence. This means you live there for the next 12 months, which is a requirement for an owner occupant loan. By doing this, you can actually get the best possible financing terms, interest rate, and down payment. After the 12 months, the loan still has the same terms from when you first signed up, but you're able to move and rent it out. You can keep living in it of course, but that option to move out is still there. A great reason for this option is the fact that you're living in this property for a whole year. You get to learn about any issues popping up and anything that needs to be fixed, and actually, have the time to do it before renting it out. Plus, if there is something that needs to be done, like any renovations, then you can do them without spending a ton of money. If you were in your own house and had to make renovations to your rental property, that would mean you'd be making double payments on two homes. That's a lot of money all at once! And as an added bonus, you'll end up being a lot more selective in the type of property you purchase. You'll invest in something that you yourself would want to live in, which means it'll probably be a higher quality than something you wouldn't stay in. The higher quality of home means higher quality of tenant. A great thing about this type of loan is that you can keep doing it over and over again. The loan terms run in yearly increments, so you can either choose 12 months, 24 months, or 36 months. Once the term is over, you can move out. When you know it's getting time to move out, then just buy another property with another owner-occupant loan and move into that one. You'll be able to rent out the first property and live in the second. Then when the term is up for the second one, you can buy a third and start the process over. You'll end up with however many homes you'd like to make rental properties, and end up making some great profits.

Straight Rental Property: Another option is buying it as a straight rental property. To go this route, you'd need a large down payment, which is why many choose the owner occupancy loan. But for those who can afford it, doing it this way means you'll be able to rent the property out pretty much right away instead of waiting one to three years. The down payment is typically 20 to 25 percent for many of the lenders, although you could possibly find some for 10 percent. But you also have to consider any extra costs, like closing and renovation. So actually, you'd need about 30 to 35 percent upfront. And for a $150,000 property, that would be $50,000 cash, upfront and all at once. In addition to that, you'd also need to make sure you have good credit and actually qualify for the lenders financing program. Of course, there are some pretty good benefits to this type of loan with rental properties. Many banks include an estimate of the net rental income, which can help your debt to income. And a lot of times rental properties can already have tenants in place, which will be very advantageous to you. If the tenants are at the rental already, you can actually get the security deposit from the person selling during closing, and even some of the pro-rated rent. Your mortgage payment is typically due a month after everything is done, so you'll be able to collect that first month's rent before having to start your mortgage payments. Plus, you're also able to make your mortgage payment due on a specific date, so you can make it after rent is due. That way, you'll get all the rent payments before having to pay your mortgage payment. Of course, there's also the added benefit of there being no vacancy, so you don't have to go through the hassle of trying to find tenants. It can be a huge pain finding someone trustworthy to rent your property, so already having people there makes things so much easier. And since there are already people living there, you probably won't have to make any renovations until after they leave. That saves hugely on the costs, and you're able to spread out what you'd be spending total on the property. There are negatives to having tenants already living in your new rental property though. You could have someone who doesn't pay on time, pays too low of a rental rate for the market, someone who just doesn't pay, or tenants who don't take care of their living space. The best way to find out is by talking to them during escrow, and deciding if you'd like to keep them or cancel their lease once it's over.

It can be very costly to take on a mortgage loan; it's raised considerably from just a few years ago. Non-owner occupant properties have high fees, even the smaller loans under $100,000. But adding everything up, including the fees, title insurance, cost of escrow, appraisal costs, etc., can be anywhere up to 5 percent. Presently, rates are pretty competitive, and it's possible to get non-owner occupant financing for under 5 percent, as long as it's a 30-year mortgage. You'd be able to lock in that low-interest rate for those 30 years, which is definitely a positive.

So where exactly do you find these loans? The best option is to meet with a few different lenders and see which loans work best for what you'd want. You can look into it in either a couple different banks, a mortgage lender, and even online lenders. Each one will have different programs and different restrictions. If you get rejected by a bank, keep trying with others. A mortgage lender might accept you when the bank won't, so don't give up. Not only that, but the loans costs and interest rates vary depending on where you go, so make sure to compare across the board.

And what about the number of properties you can afford? Credit score is key here, so if you have a good one, plus good debt-to-income ratio, then you can probably finance up to about 4 different properties. Your debt-to-income ratio changes with each property, so keep that in mind too. It's possible to try even more than 4 properties, but you won't have a large number of lenders willing to help you finance. They are definitely some out there, but you'll have to look a little harder. Over 10 loans are even more difficult, but it's possible. There are lenders that specifically work with those who want over 10 loans, and they're called portfolio lenders.

Chapter 9: What are the Risks Involved?

There are definitely advantages to investing in rental properties. You can earn a lot of passive income and make great profits, all while maintaining financial security for the future. And while owning rental properties can be relatively safe, there are risks involved. It's good to practice diligence and ensure that if any of the negatives happen, you'll know how to turn it around quickly, before losing any money.

Vacancy: Having a high amount of vacancies is probably one of the worst things to happen to a rental property owner. Tenants are how you make your money and income, so going without them means you go without money. You can even reach a negative cash flow, meaning you have to start paying out of pocket for expenses. That can add up, and you end up losing a ton of money that you won't be able to make back. The best way to avoid this from happening, or at least lessen the blow is by purchasing rental properties in good neighborhoods. Do the proper research about the different areas; figure out which neighborhoods are safest, and which ones yield the best amenities. It might end up being a little more expensive to buy a property in a better neighborhood, but tenants are more likely to rent where they feel safe and where they have a lot of different things to choose from. Keeping a savings specifically for vacancies would probably be the smart thing to do, just in case you end up having to pay the mortgage, insurance, and property taxes from your own money.

Bad Tenants: While dealing with vacancies can mean you might lose money, having bad tenants can be so much worse. There's a large risk when taking in unknown people, and it requires you to be pretty selective. You need to do background checks, get references from previous landlords, ask for proof of income, run a credit check, and make sure to take a security deposit. If you end up with the wrong tenant, it could cost you a lot more than having the room empty for a bit. Make sure you also listen to what your gut is telling you. A person could be great on paper; have the necessary paperwork, have a great credit, and great references. But if there's just something odd about them, and they're giving you a strange vibe, then there might be something off about them that would mean they're not a good tenant. Trust yourself!

Cash Flow: Triple check the expenses and how much everything will cost you; even put in the cost of random maintenance that might actually never happen. Underestimating the cost could mean the end of your business and you owing thousands. Having the right team to help can make sure you don't accidentally forget something, but ultimately, it's up to you to remember. And it's not just considering the upfront costs, but how much everything will cost you each month. If you end up losing money every month because of not realizing the cost, you'll eventually be out of business from paying out of pocket.

The Right Time to Buy: Just like in other markets, the real estate market also has a sort of supply and demand. There's a constant fluctuate, so if you're thinking of maybe selling your property down the road, you might end up not making a profit. Investing in rental properties can cost a lot of money, especially up front, so you want to make sure that your expected return in the future makes is actually worth making the investment in the first place. The best thing to do is see if it's a seller's or buyer's market, and keep up with the trends. You want to buy in a buyer's market and sell once it's circled back around to a seller's market.

Theft: There's always a risk of your property becoming burglarized, especially if you're in a lower income location. If the crime rate is on the higher side, then you'll end up with a high turnover of tenants. Plus, what you charge for rent will be much lower than what you could charge in a higher income location. If burglary does happen a lot in your location, you could end up paying a lot of money in legal procedures and fees.

Foreclosure: If you end up not making enough profit, and can't meet your mortgage payments, then there's the change of your property being foreclosed. That's definitely the last thing you want because not only can it hurt you being approved for any future real estate loans, but word might get around, and no one would want to rent from you. Knowing the numbers and making sure you'll get a profit can help minimize the chance, plus making sure you have an emergency savings to help you out if needed.

Maintenance: Especially at the beginning, before you hire someone, you'll probably be the person your tenants call when something goes wrong. There's a high level of work involved when running rental properties, and that included maintenance issues. What happens when a pipe bursts? You can't just let it sit and hope it fixes itself. And if it happens in the middle of the night, there's a high chance that you won't be able to get anyone out to fix it until the next morning. Knowing basic maintenance can be very helpful as a landlord, and help you to save spending more money on issues that end up becoming a lot worse. Or if you're not very handy, you can hire a property manager that does know how to fix those types of thing. Keep in mind too that eventually, properties start to show their age. They typically start having structural damage, and major things would need replacing. It's best to keep up with everything, because if you let it go, then it'll just get worse and cost you a lot more money than necessary.

Airbnb: There's actually some risk to renting out property specifically for short-term rent, like Airbnb. You can make a lot of money doing it, but sometimes the local authorities put forth certain laws and restrictions for these types of businesses. You have to make sure that you pay all the different fees and taxes, and learn all the different local state and city laws about short-term rentals. Make sure to keep up with it because some laws might change and you could get into trouble if you don't change with them.

Chapter 10: How to Manage Your Properties

You basically have two options when it comes to managing your rental properties. You can either do it all yourself or hire a management company. Both have pros and cons, and it's really up to you with what works best for your style and business. A lot of the work and issues are at the beginning of the process when you're actually buying the property, which is good news. Basically, there's less work involved after getting the property, keep in mind that it still does take work. There's a specific process that goes into managing a rental, and each thing is handled differently depending on whether it's you or a management company.

Pre-Rent Repairs: It's always best to go around the property and determine what needs to be fixed before you even rent your property out. This is probably something that just you will be dealing with because typically property managers help with maintenance only after the property is rented. Knowing what kind of repairs the property needs and how much it's all going to cost is good to know even before buying the property, but you'll be able to get a better idea of how much work it will take once you do the walkthrough.

How Much is Rent: Knowing how much to rent the property for is determined by location, how much the house is worth, and how much you need in income. But what number you come up with might be different than the number a management company comes up with. A property manager wants to rent the property as quickly as possible because they collect their money based off of the rent. However, doing this might mean the property manager rents it for less than what it's worth, and you'll end up not making as much as you need.

Renting: Renting out the property can be a difficult process and frankly a little tedious. You need to find tenants, ones that you know will be good and make you the most money possible. That involves putting out advertisements for the property, showing your home, checking their credit, running a background check, creating a contract and lease, and collecting their money. You might start feeling frustrated and end up picking the tenant because they're the first to show up or they're the only ones willing to pay your asking price. You just have to remember to think in long run terms and remember that having patience when finding the right tenant will be worth it. Of course, this is where have a property manager comes in handy. You can let them know your specifications, and then leave everything in their hands. They can take care of the nitty gritty while you sit back and relax!

Money: It's very important that your tenants pay on time. You have mortgage payments to keep up with, and if they're late then your late. That reflects much worse on you then it does on them, so it's up to you to enforce timely payments. The best way to do this is by having late fees. And late fees are something you need to keep up with and be strict about. If you let one person slide, then everyone else will think it's ok. You might hear sob story after sob story, but you need to be firm and hold your ground. You might even have to start the eviction process if the tenant is very late, which could be the wake-up call they need. If you're the type of person that is very compassionate or kind-hearted then it would probably be best to utilize a property manager for this process. They can be your go-between and collect the rent for you. It's their job to make sure the rent is collected on time and in full, so they would be perfectly fine with a harsher attitude and implementing the late fees.

Eviction: It's definitely a horrible process, and there are bad feelings all around when you have to evict a tenant. It's not something you like doing, and you risk the possibility of the tenant turning on you when you evict them. They might even take it out on you by trashing your property, which is the last thing you'd want to deal with. It's best to try to get a tenant to move out on good terms, so you don't have to worry about the room being messed up or dealing with what's owed. Just like collecting rent, if you'd rather not deal with the annoyance and hassle of evicting someone, a property management company can be a big help. You can leave the evictions up to them and not have to deal with upset or angry tenants. This is especially nice if you're worried about your safety; having another person with you when you're evicting someone is just good common sense.

Keep up with your houses: Even though you have a tenant, it's a good idea to do a walk through every once in a while. Your tenant might say they're keeping up with the house, but you really don't know unless you actually go over and look. The best way to do this without your tenant getting upset from you "invading" is by writing it in the lease. You can put in there that you have the right to do a property inspection at any time, as long as there's notice given. Most of the time, the notice is either 24 to 48 hours. That gives the tenant enough time to clean up anything they'd want to but not enough to hide any major issues. You can utilize this time to ensure that the property is being maintained well, check the smoke detectors and change the batteries if needed, and check to see if there are any other repairs needed. Many times, the biggest issues that happen are due to landlords who actually never check on their rental property. The tenant is paying on time every month and never seems to cause any problems, so that means the house is fine, right? Not exactly! The tenant could be on their best behavior because they're actually not keeping up with the house and destroying it. The worst kind of damage happens over a long period of time; a constant drip, an animal soiling the carpet, etc. Or maybe the tenant is doing something illegal and doesn't want you checking on the property for fear of being found out. If you really want to know what's going on in your house, then you should keep checking on it periodically yourself. You can hire a property manager, but they could just tell you they went to check on the house and never actually did it. You can never be completely sure unless you do it yourself. If you'd prefer a property manager though, then that's perfectly fine, but make sure to do a walk through at least once a month just to double check.

Maintenance: This isn't just something that happens during the pre-renting phase. As long as you have a property, then you'll need to do maintenance on it. Things will always break or need replacing, and it can be a lot of work to keep up with. You don't want properties that are broken down and obviously need a lot of work; tenants don't want to live in a place that has broken windows. To keep up with the maintenance issues, you should plan ahead for them by accounting them into your expense plan. That way, if something does happen then, it's completely fine because you've already planned for it. That's especially pertinent when there's water or electrical issues. You don't want your basement flooding because you couldn't afford to replace the pipes. These issues can happen at any time, and anywhere on your property, so you need to be prepared for that. Being prepared includes taking calls at 3 in the morning because of that pipe bursting. But if you prefer your sleep, that's where a property manager comes in handy. Instead of going to you about maintenance issues, the tenant can just call your property manager, and they can handle it. Obviously, they'll contact you if any work needs to be done, but it's nice to have a go-between taking care of the more difficult issues.

Legalese: It's important to keep track of all your expenses, rent amounts, profits, losses, etc. And if you're great at that sort of thing, then feel free to take it on! But having a property manager handle it all instead of you is pretty nice and means you don't have to worry about keeping track of everything. They can compile it all, and send it off to your accountant for review. You let them handle the dirty work and reap the benefits.

If you do decide to go with a property manager, remember to put that expense in your start-up costs. They can cut into what your profit will be, but keep in mind everything they'll do for you in return. They typically take around 8 to 12 percent of whatever the monthly rents add up to be, which really isn't that bad. Of course, when you're first starting out, usually it's with only one or two properties. Unless you're just extremely busy and have a lot of other stuff going on, then you probably don't need a property manager. But as you acquire more and more rental properties, then it would definitely make sense to hire some help. Think about it like this - if you are only renting out one property, then usually it takes only about a few hours every month to manage it, besides the process of finding tenants. You'll have to deal with collecting your rent, maintenance issues, and other small things, all which don't really add up too much time away from your day to day life. Even adding on another property or two still doesn't really take up that much time. However, once you've reached 4 or more rental properties, then that's when you begin to become overwhelmed. You might end up skimping out on the screening process for tenants or decide to slack on checking on your properties in person, both of which can cause you to lose some serious money. If you find yourself becoming overwhelmed and overworked, then get help in the form of a property manager. It's definitely worth that small fee for peace of mind and freedom of time.

Chapter 11: How to Know When to Exit

There might come a time when you're ready to sell your rental property. It makes sense to keep it long term, and there are many benefits to actually never selling. But maybe you're tired of dealing with tenants and repair issues, maybe it's a good time to sell, and you'd like to make a nice profit. Or maybe you just want to get out of the game. Regardless of your reasoning, there are some very specific factors to take into consideration when you realize it's time to sell your rental property:

Life: It happens, we get it. You can have a major life event, something that makes you reconsider owning your properties. Maybe a family member died, maybe you were laid off and no longer have the right funds to help support yourself, maybe you have to move across the country. You end up spending a lot of time and money focusing on whatever event is happening, so much so that you just don't have time to deal with your properties. It's possible that you can sell all of them, or maybe just downsize to one or two, enough for a little passive income.

More Money: It's entirely possible that you end up making a lot more money elsewhere. You could have another revenue source that really took off, or maybe you have a full-time job that just offered a great promotion. Rental income is considered passive income, but it also takes a lot of effort. If you can get more money from somewhere else that takes less effort, then it makes a lot more sense to go with that other option.

Not Enough Money: While you'd love if everyone loves your property, you have amazing tenants and are making a great income each month, there's a chance that you could end up with a negative cash flow instead. When investing in rentals, it's important to be making an income off of them in the first month. If you've gone months without any profits, and in fact are in the negatives, then maybe it's time to reevaluate this property and whether it's worth it.

Unhappy: Maybe you're just unhappy with how things are in your life now. You were excited about investing in rental properties at first, but now it's just too much work with no reward. Why would you keep doing something that makes you unhappy? Being a landlord can be a stressful job. That stress might be something you overlook because you're making great money and getting amazing profits. But eventually, it can become a burden and weigh pretty heavy on you. You end up with a ton of anxiety and stress that never really goes away. And not only is that a lot to deal with, but it's also extremely bad for your health! You don't want a heart attack just because you're unhappy in your job, do you?

Too Much: Real estate is all about supply and demand. If there are too many houses on the market, then the selling price will go down. That's definitely something you'd like to avoid, but it might be inevitable. While houses are sold and bought all the time, if there are new homes being built then it will be a very long time before it's a seller's market. Housing for sale or rent will become oversaturated and flooded. If you notice that there are a ton of new houses or condos being built, it's best to sell before they're finished, or you'll end up having to wait until it comes back around. Which could take decades, so you need to figure out if you want to keep renting that long or not.

Taxes: Property taxes are a pain. They can cause a lot of hassle and upset feelings, and they're something the local and state governments keep increasing instead of going somewhere else. Basically, if the local government has a big project in the works, like filling in all the potholes, they just decide to raise property taxes instead of increasing road tolls. This means that with higher property taxes, then the rent increases as well. The issue with this though is that increasing rent takes some time. It might say on your lease that you can't raise rent until the lease is over. And if that's not for another 8 months, then that's 8 months that you'll have to pay property taxes out of your own pocket. If you start seeing this trend happen a lot in your current city, it might make more sense to move to a state that is tax friendly. Fun fact, but Hawaii is actually the best state for dealing with property tax. It's ranked #50 at 0.28 percent, which means you'll be paying the lowest possible property tax out of all the states. Renting out a property as an Airbnb on Hawaii would probably be a great idea!

Commercial Real Estate: A great way to figure out whether or not residential housing is growing is by looking at how the commercial real estate scene is. Companies need to find a workspace before hiring people, so houses typically come second when there's about to be a big boom. You can look at this information and learn if there's a real estate slowdown happening. If companies aren't buying space in your area, then people probably aren't looking to move there any time soon.

Major Repairs: There are typical large expenses that happen like clockwork - a roof needs to be replaced every 10 to 20 years, a new water heater every 10 to 15 years, etc. These are normal, and you'll figure them into your housing costs at the beginning of the buying process. However, it's possible your property ends up needing repairs that cost more than it's worth. A law was recently passed in San Francisco that meant any housing units over a garage had to be retrofitted, which costs anywhere from $100,000 to $300,000. That's a lot of money to spend all at once, or even in a payment plan. You need to assess your property and decide if it's worth fixing or worth more just to sell it.

Natural Disasters: Does your area have any natural disasters? Specific areas can be more susceptible to things like flooding, fires, hurricanes, etc. It's best to research your area and figure out which natural disaster is the norm and how often it hits. Hurricanes hit the Gulf coast every year, but the really deadly ones only hit every 5 to 10 years. If you know, it's been a few years since a disaster has struck, or if you have decided to opt out of the natural disaster insurance, then maybe it's a good idea to sell. You could end up losing your house and be left with the land, in which it would be very expensive to try and rebuild.

Commission Rates: The commission rate for real estate agents has been steady at a very high 5 percent, which isn't much of a difference from the 6 percent that was ten years ago! The main issue is that half of the 5 percent, 2.5 percent, goes to the buyer's real estate agent. They obviously want the best possible deal for their client, which means the best possible deal for them. You're basically paying the buyer's real estate agent instead of their own client. And most real estate agents try to find listings that have the 2.5 percent commission, so if yours doesn't, then it will be doubly difficult to sell. If by some chance the commission rate goes down, then take the chance before it changes again by selling.

Appreciate the Property: There is such a thing as the property having "appreciation." This is when the value of the property goes up, and it becomes worth it to sell. Let's say you decide to invest in a fixer-upper for your rental property. You completely overhaul it; new furniture, new appliances, new everything. Your plan is to rent it out, and you're successfully making a great profit from it. However, there's a chance that because the property is so great now, and if the location becomes more up and coming and hip, then the value of the property goes way up. When that happens, you need to decide whether you'd like to keep renting it out or sell it. If you do sell, you could use some of that money to put back into a different property instead.

Conclusion

Thank you for making it through to the end of *Rental Property Investing: How to Create Wealth and Passive Income Through Intelligent Real Estate Investing*. Let's hope it was informative and able to provide you with all of the tools you need to achieve your goals whatever they may be.

The next step is to figure out where you go from here. It might be best to start slow, maybe even speak to several real estate investors for their opinions and how they got started. Or you could just jump right in and start researching properties and their locations. Remember, location is everything to your success, so it's best to look up several properties and then look around at the different amenities they have. You could even do it opposite; if there's an area that you really like and know will do really well, look up if there are any properties for sale in it. Look at apartments, single family homes, and multi-family homes to see which ones you'd prefer and which ones would do the best in the area you're interested in. And don't forget, you can look at the properties first, but make sure your direct next step is figuring out exactly how much you can afford. You'll need to know the exact number you're fine with spending in closing costs so that you know what to do when negotiating. There's a lot of work that goes into real estate investing, especially when it's rentals. But this book can really help you figure things out without getting overwhelmed and truly help you to succeed.

Finally, if you found this book useful in any way, a review on Amazon is always appreciated!

www.ingramcontent.com/pod-product-compliance
Lightning Source LLC
Chambersburg PA
CBHW030504220526
45464CB00006B/2650